Sowing in Tears

Sowing in Tears

*A Mother's Sorrow in Infertility
and Joy in Adoption*

LEEANN HALE

Website—https://www.facebook.com/sowingintearsbook
Email—sowingintearsbook@gmail.com

Table of Contents

Adoption symbol: Each point of the triangle represents the birth-parents, adoptive parents and the adoptee. The heart surrounding the triangle represents the love that unites them.

Acknowledgments

I would like to begin by thanking some influential people who held our hands throughout our journey. First, and foremost, God's sovereign hand was, and still is, at work in every part of my life. He held us when we were broken and He rejoiced with us in our victories. He is the only One who could change a heart and mindset so completely and drastically, and He is the only one who could bless me far more than I ever asked or thought. If you do not know or have a personal relationship with the God who created all things from nothing and came to die the most cruel and gruesome death so He could be a sacrifice for our sinful souls, ask me. My God is Healer of the broken and He alone is mighty to save. I'd love to tell you more about my Heavenly Father, and how He can be yours too.

I'd like to thank my husband who faithfully stood by my side in the lowest parts of our valley and in our highest mountaintop experiences. He was steady in his love towards me and abundantly faithful in following God's leading. I wouldn't have wanted anyone else by my side though our trials. The godly example he shows as head of our household is a treasure I too often take for granted. His love and passion for the Lord have humbled me many times, and much of the growth in my adult Christian walk with my Savior is a testament to a husband who seeks to honor and glorify God with his heart, soul, mind and strength.

To my boys: may your lives forever be a testament to God's love and faithfulness. You both have changed my life in ways you will never fully understand. Jayden, you gave me the name I longed to be called: Mom. Jaxon, you were not far behind in reminding me that God's plans are far better than my own. You both were the result of countless prayers. You have also multiplied my responsibilities, stripped from me countless hours of sleep, seen me broken and weary, but most importantly, given me a joy I never knew existed. You genuinely make me laugh, smile and love more than I knew I could. Jayden, you melt my heart when you recite scripture in your small, toddler voice and when you sing praises to Jesus at the top of your lungs. Both your lives, though they haven't seen many years, have touched the hearts of many. Before you were even born, I prayed for you fervently, and I loved you deeply before you ever reached my arms. As we always say before we tuck you into bed, "Mommy loves you, Daddy loves you, Jesus loves you MOST!"

I would like to thank the brave and courageous women who carried my boys into this world. To Jayden's birthparents: although we've never met in person, you both will always hold a special place in my heart. Our short text conversation just a couple of weeks after we brought Jayden home is permanently saved in my phone. Your words meant more to me than you will ever know, and Jayden will grow to know the deep love you have for him in giving him the life you thought was best for him. To Jaxon's birthmother: my love towards you started before our first hug, and it didn't end with our last. You are one of the strongest women I have ever met. I treasure our relationship and look forward to sharing more memories with you. We are so proud of you for all your accomplishments, and Jax will always know that he is your inspiration for all you do. Each night when we say prayers with the boys, we pray specifically for you three. We pray that the Lord would keep you safe wherever your life takes you, and that you would be drawn closer to Him and know His saving grace. Love is brave!

To our adoption agency and our attorney: words can't express my gratitude for all you did to help us become a family. You poured in time, above and beyond what was expected of you, and you showed genuine love and care for us all through each step. God led us to both of you at different times and for that I will forever be grateful.

To the Giugliano and Riley families: I didn't have a clue where to start or where to begin; I only knew God was leading us to adoption. You paved the way and answered all my questions, and your testimonies thrilled my heart. Your love for the Lord shines brightly in your lives and I'm thankful for the guidance you provided and the prayers you prayed alongside us through our journey.

To all our extended family and our church family: you all amazed us with your generosity. You gave sacrificially of your time, finances, prayers and—most importantly—your love in welcoming our boys home. Many of you prayed daily throughout our journey and that is, I believe, why we experienced the peace that surpasses all human understanding. We love you all and are honored that you have come alongside us to be part of the village that it takes to raise our children.

And to my beta readers who read my book in its very early stages, my publishing company, and my editor, Amy Clutter: you are the real champions. You suffered through pages full of errors, lack of detail, and grammatical inconsistencies; you are a huge part of why this book is all that it is now. You encouraged me to continue pressing on and writing what God laid on my heart to write, and I thank you so much for your insight and wisdom during the editing process.

Dedication

To all the birthmothers who may be reading this, your courage is inspiring. The pain you endure, both physically and emotionally, is not in vain. Every child is a gift from God. Each one uniquely known, fearfully and wonderfully made, and formed in your womb by the Creator of the universe. He is the Giver of life, and you are the vessel He chose to bring that life into existence. You are loved and never forgotten. There is no shame for your actions, but there is victory because there is hope. There is hope for adoptive parents longing to welcome a baby into their home, there is hope for the child to have a life and future without limitations, and there is hope for you because there is One who knows the deepest parts of your hurt and suffering. He alone is the Healer. You are loved because you, too, are a gift.

To all the adoptive parents who may have walked a similar path to us, or may be right in the thick of it now, keep pushing and keep the faith. Do not be discouraged. God truly writes the best stories for our good and His glory. He is the greatest author of our lives and when you give your life to Him and trust Him to order your steps, He will show Himself faithful.

And to the greatest treasure and gift to both of the above sets of people, you, sweet child, are loved. Your parents chased hard after you. They loved you before they met you, and your life is a testament of God's answer to prayer. Adoption isn't an easy path, but *you* were worth the wait. No matter the history of your birthparents, whether good or bad circumstances, they chose life. They chose *you*. They may have made mistakes leading up to that point, but they didn't give up on you. Even more than your parents and birthparents, God held you in the palm of His hands from the instant you were conceived, and He is holding you still. His greatest desire is for His children to follow Him. You have the unique ability to reach people most can't. Your story is special, and so are you. Give your life to Jesus and let Him take you places far better than you could think or imagine. Whether life causes you, at times, to sow in tears or reap with shouts of joy, there is no better place to be than held in the arms of Jesus. As a child of the King, you are chosen, you are protected, and you are loved!

Jayden Jonas and Jaxon Korbyn, shine bright for Jesus in all you do. I love you with all my heart.

Preface

My hope in writing this book is that I would be able to use the beautiful story God designed for my life to help others. In doing so, I feel I need to be completely transparent and vulnerable. I decided if I wanted to share my story, I couldn't just pick and choose the parts I wanted people to see. I had to also choose the parts that I was ashamed of, because God in His sovereignty used all the parts to create our beautiful love story. As Christians, we too often feel the need to sugarcoat our life. We think if we don't seem like we have it all together, we will be judged. If all the words out of our mouths and all the thoughts and intents of our hearts were perfect—knowing no sin—we would have no need for a perfect Savior to take the form of a man and come to earth to die on the cross for our sins.

The title of my book came from Psalm 126:5: "Those who sow in tears shall reap with shouts of joy!" (English Standard Version). My desire for you, my reader, is that you would be able to see the clear transition from hopelessness in Part One to hope in Christ in Part Two. Part One is a glimpse back to my prideful and selfish heart. I knew Jesus held the plans for my future, but I didn't fully believe His ways were better than my ways. In Part Two, you will see my heart change as I learn to trust Christ and His sovereignty over every part of our journey, even during our infertility.

My life is far from perfect. I fail as a wife, mother, daughter, sister, friend—the list could go on and on—but my God remains a faithful God. I wrote this book, often with tears in my eyes, because I can't imagine my path to motherhood playing out any other way. Adoption is a beautiful picture of God adopting us as His children, and Zach and I cannot wait to share with our boys their adoption story as they grow. I thank God that His plans were far better than my plans. I often think of my boys' birthmothers and how brave and strong they were. I think of how they chose life in the midst of their pain and fears. They were brave when courage felt fleeting. And they were strong when hope seemed dim.

The testimony of my boys has touched countless people, and I cannot wait to see what God has in store as they grow older. I never knew a joy unspeakable until Zach and I set out on the journey to find them. I thank God for changing my ugly heart and graciously handing me my precious little 5 lb 13 oz blessing on November 11, 2016, making me a mother for the first time.

Part One: Sowing in Tears

Hear my cry, O God, listen to my prayer; from the end of the earth I call to you when my heart is faint.

(Psalm 61:1-2a, ESV)

1

Diagnosis

⌀

December 28, 2014. We had finally decided on a date! For the past few months I had been getting baby fever to the extreme, and getting my planner husband to agree to try to start a family with me was becoming more of a challenge than I had anticipated. However, it was Christmas break, and whether it was my well-practiced, incessant pestering, or simply the joy-filled holiday season, he was ready! We could officially start trying to get pregnant! Zach would graduate from physical therapy school in five months, and it would be perfect timing for me to stop teaching and stay at home with our baby. *Wow! This will be my last year of teaching! Only five more months and I will be pregnant through the summer and our baby will be here next fall!*

The last of my papers were graded, report cards were sent home, and my classroom was all packed up for summer break. Five months had passed and I was in the same position that I had been in December. I knew people said it could take up to a year to become pregnant, but no part of me really thought that's how it would happen for *us*. Still, I was left with no signs of morning sickness—oh, how I longed to just wake up one morning puking my guts out! Every minor inconsistency—even a bad cough—would get typed into Google in hopes of it being a pregnancy symptom. Unfortunately, thanks to the Internet,

3

every little symptom can somehow be linked to pregnancy these days; but mine were just that: a scratchy throat, an itch on my foot, and a headache. No pregnancy attached.

Why is this not working? I didn't understand what could possibly be wrong. Dashed hopes and negative pregnancy tests continued to haunt me month after month.

The pages of the calendar flipped by. Months came and went and it was now November of 2015, so I made an appointment with my OB/GYN. Surely, we would get some answers and figure out what was taking so long. I remember that particular day was filled with excitement. I took a half day off from work, and on the drive to the doctor's office I just knew I would be given some good news. Actually, I thought I might be a couple of days late for my period, and the nurse thought it was a good idea to take a pregnancy test before going into my room. *Yes!* I was hoping she would suggest that. I was starting to love pregnancy tests. I already started planning how I would surprise Zach with the news. Since I had a half day off work anyway, I knew I would be home before him. I could stop by the store and get a "Daddy" card, maybe some balloons—

"It's negative," said the nurse.

Well, of course it's negative! It's been negative for a year, why would it be anything else? It's okay, nothing is going to get in the way of this doctor's appointment, not even a negative pregnancy test. Sometimes it's too early to tell anyway. I'll probably take another test in a week just to double-check.

"You can undress and the doctor will be with you shortly," the nurse explained as she motioned me to my room.

As I sat waiting, I fought back the tears. This was all becoming a very emotional process. *Wait, crying a lot—isn't that a pregnancy symptom? I bet that test was just taken too soon. The directions say to take them with first morning urine* (FMU—I was becoming very familiar with fertility acronyms). *I'll try another test in the morning.*

The doctor walked in the room and I explained everything: my health, my menstrual cycles, and my desire to start a family but being unsuccessful for a year. I had a detailed list of when we started trying to conceive, how long my cycles were lasting, and the lengths of my periods. This information was all very easy to share because as soon as we started trying, I downloaded a pregnancy tracker app on my phone. I had so much fun entering all the information month after month, and it made it easy for a day like today when the doctor was asking a lot of questions. I felt like a well-prepared student on test day. I was totally acing this test.

The doctor suggested that I get some blood work and have a trans-vaginal ultrasound done to see if anything peculiar showed up on the tests. She also referred Zach to a fertility doctor to get a semen analysis to check for any inconsistencies or abnormalities in his health.

A few days passed and we both received follow-up calls from our doctors. Zach's test showed everything was great on his end and there was no problem at all. My tests showed similar results and there was nothing in either of us that seemed to be out of the ordinary.

"Unexplained infertility," I was told. *I waited a year for that diagnosis?!* I had read the *infertility* word quite a bit now in all my personal research, but never had it been linked with my name: Leeann Hale— unexplained *infertility*. Now the word seemed to have such a different meaning. It was a dirty word. I felt like the label was plastered on my forehead for all to see. This really wasn't the news I was expecting. *How does a diagnosis that begins with the word "unexplained" help? If they don't know why I have this problem, how can they even begin to fix this problem?*

2
The Best Problem

I t was now December 2015, exactly a year from when we first started trying to become pregnant. It was amazing how different my emotions were. A year before, I was gung-ho and jumping for joy at the thought of starting a family. Flash forward to today: my desires hadn't changed, but a sense of sadness now followed me everywhere I went.

We were given the option of trying Clomid, a medication used to help stimulate ovulation. This was something I had read about and was very excited to try. This obviously would work, and I was hoping it might work *too* well. In a lot of my readings, women who were prescribed Clomid often had multiples. That would be awesome! I was starting to believe God was going to give me twins because of how long I've had to wait.

The first two failed cycles of Clomid were hard, but nothing as hard as the third and final failed cycle, because now we weren't advised to continue. We weren't exactly advised *not* to try a fourth round, but we were encouraged—and I had also done some personal research that made me hesitant—to move forward in a different direction. Back to square one. I had such high hopes for that medication. I had been getting genuinely excited for twins. I had their nursery all planned out in my head, little matching outfits—*I can't think about that now! It's too hard. I keep opening YouTube and watching pregnancy announcements. Why do I do this? I guess it gives me something to look forward to or gives me another reason to cry in my bed. Probably a little of both.*

On March 9, 2016, we were referred to fertility specialists. Thankfully the fertility clinic was not too far from us: a 45-minute to an hour drive, depending on traffic. So much anticipation was built on this specific meeting. Zach and I both took the morning off work to attend the initial consultation together. The thought of exiting our car and taking the first step into the building was exciting, but it was also very nerve-racking. As we sat in the waiting room, I looked around. The room was gorgeous and everything looked so fancy to me, but I still felt extremely uncomfortable as we sat and waited for our names to be called. Looking around the room, my eyes bounced from infertility posters to parent magazines to what I called—and what now applied to me—"lonely couples." We all knew we were here for the same reason. Something was wrong with us and we couldn't get pregnant. We all required specialized help. I felt like we were the misfits on the Island of Misfit Toys.

My eyes darted to the entrance. A couple walked in with their child. Yes, you read that correctly: their *child.* What reason could they possibly have to come here? It was very obvious that this whole fertility thing had worked for them. Seeing that little girl all snuggled up close in her mother's arms was so crushing, yet I remember smiling and waving as I made eye contact with the toddler in beautiful, curly, blonde pigtails. I wished so badly that I was the one holding her. I couldn't believe I was sitting in this waiting room. This was never part of my plan for parenthood.

"Zach and Leeann," called the nurse.

We were escorted down to the doctor's office. He had a new diagnosis for me: polycystic ovary syndrome (PCOS). *Hey, I already like this guy. He's telling me something I don't know. PCOS doesn't sound good, but it sounds a whole lot better than unexplained infertility.*

"...This is actually the best problem to come to us with," he continued.

Oh, wow! Now I really like this guy. A good problem, one they can fix easily. This is great! For the next half hour or so he went on to explain my problem with an immense amount of medical terms. I was nodding and shaking my head in agreement while on the inside very thankful for a husband who has his doctorate degree in the medical field—*I'll just ask for a translation in the car.* After our meeting with him, we met his personal nurse and then a financial advisor. This was all a lot more complex than what I had envisioned. We were now officially "fertility specialist patients," and we were the only ones who knew.

Even now, people still ask us why we never said anything for so long, why we insisted on keeping this news to ourselves. Even though at that point it had been over a year, it still didn't ever really *feel* like we had this problem. I was living in denial often. Looking back, it would have been a lot easier to just come out and say it, but in the moment, it seemed like the worst possible move. Unfortunately, that meant we would continue to have to answer the questions: *"When are you going to start having kids?" "Maybe Leeann's pregnant?" "Do you guys want kids?"* These were all well-meaning people, but these weren't the questions

I wanted to answer at the time. Sure, back in the first few years of our marriage those had been fun to answer, but certainly not now.

I didn't want to tell family because I didn't want to have to start back at the beginning; it would be too hard to relive crushed hopes over and over. If I just waited a little bit longer, we could share the news at the same time we shared a pregnancy announcement. That sounded like the best option!

We'll keep it to ourselves just a little longer.

3
Follicle Counting

◇

*T*hese pills are for the birds! I was careful about the food I ate with them like the doctor said, but they were still messing with my stomach on a daily basis. Do you know the feeling when you think you're going to throw up, but you never actually do? Every morning that was what it felt like. *Stupid Metformin! The doctor wants me to try to work up to three pills a day. He's crazy! I'm only on two right now; if he thinks he's going to get me to add another one to my already messed up morning routine, he's lost his mind.*

On the bright side, I'm excited for the self-injections. Is that weird to say? I'm excited to stick myself with needles! The idea of shots made me feel like we would actually be doing something, like we were actually moving in a forward direction. Unfortunately, I still had to wait until the end of my cycle before I could start, which wouldn't be for another few weeks. When the time came, I would be able to make my appointments in the mornings before school at a location closer to home. This would save me gas and time, which was becoming very important because of how often I needed to be seen.

Walking up to the door for my first checkup was exhilarating. It was an odd waiting room, and when I walked in, it was like I entered a ghost town. No one was there. My eyes were immediately drawn to another door leading to what I assumed was a whole new set of rooms. I could hear people talking on the other side of the door. Plastered on the door was a sign that read, "Do not open, we will be with you shortly." Of course, I couldn't hold back my anticipation so I opened the door.

Cheryl greeted me with a big smile. "You must be Leeann. I will be right with you once I finish up with this patient. You can go have a seat in the waiting room."

I walked back with my head hanging in embarrassment. At least now she knew I was here. *Why did I have to open the door? Why couldn't I have just obeyed the sign like any normal person? How awkward! Hey, don't mind me over here, just a reading teacher who apparently doesn't know how to read.* I was getting in my head now. *Just calm down,* I tried to tell myself.

I was in the process of reading through the Bible in a year, so I decided to use this time to pull out my phone and see what chapters were scheduled for today's reading. I started reading while I waited for Cheryl to come get me.

"Alright Leeann, I'm ready for you," Cheryl welcomed me with a side hug and another huge smile. *I think she's going to be my favorite.*

She walked me into the first room where I would get a taste of what most of my mornings would look like from now on. She started with drawing my blood. I don't really have a problem with needles, but I also didn't have the overwhelming desire to stare as she poked me. I decided it would be best if I just stared a hole in the ground. After getting my blood drawn and using the restroom, Cheryl led me to the exam room where I would be getting my ultrasound. She told me to take my bottoms off, hop up on the table, and use the paper cloth to drape over my lap and she would be in shortly.

As I sat there waiting, I realized I left my shoes right in front of the doorway for her to trip over when she came in. I contemplated getting up and moving them, but at that point I had been sitting in the room awhile; she was probably about to come in at any second. I certainly didn't want to be standing half-naked in the doorway when she walked in!

I guess I'll just leave them. Or maybe I should just get up. Yes. I'll get up. I'm fast. I can scoot right off the table, kick the shoes to the side and she'll never even realize.

Completely interrupting my thoughts, in walked Cheryl and, of course, tripped over my shoes. She kindly moved them to the seat and I apologized, avoiding eye contact. *What a great first impression I am making today. Not!*

The ultrasound was not the most relaxing feeling I've ever experienced, but she showed me the monitor as she was looking, and it distracted me from the discomfort. She began to explain that she was looking for follicles. *What's a follicle?* I probably should have known this, but I didn't, so I asked. She then went on to explain everything so carefully and in terms that I could understand. My follicles—which I learned were the means to carry and release my eggs for fertilization—were too small to measure at this point, but I could see them. She checked both my left and right side. She took the time to point each one out so I could begin to understand this whole process. I was fascinated with what was going on inside me.

As I understood it, my problem before seeking treatment was that my body was making too many follicles. You would think that would be a good thing, right? Well, it wasn't. Too many follicles meant they took up too much space and, in turn, weren't able to grow to the greatest possible size to allow fertilization to take place. Don't take this report to a medical doctor because I'm sure I'm not using the correct terminology, but in my head at the time, it was starting to come together and make some sense. This was the start of follicle counting with Cheryl. There would be many more visits and much more counting in my future.

April 21, 2016: tonight was the big night! It was time for my first shot: Gonal-*f* RFF Redi-ject (follitropin alfa injection). *What a name, right?!* I was excited and nervous all at the same time. I practiced with Cheryl a couple times that morning just to make sure I knew what I was doing. We used a stress ball as the injection site in place of my stomach. She showed me how to pinch my stomach and adjust the dial on the pen to make sure the correct amount of medication was injected properly. The doctor gave instructions to start out on the lowest dosage amount. *How annoying.* Cheryl said he does this so he can monitor me on the first cycle and see what would be an appropriate dose for next time. *Just give me the highest dose!* was what I wanted to say.

"Oh, ok, that makes sense," was what I actually said.

I had to pick a consistent time in the evening because the timing of the shots was important. I later found out that I probably had an hour of wiggle room, but even if I had known that at the time, I still would have stuck to the exact time on the minute to give us the best possible chance of success. I picked later in the evening in case we ever had plans that kept us out later. The time was chosen: 9 p.m. When I got home from work, it seemed I was counting down the seconds. Finally, the time came. I got the medicine from the refrigerator and dialed 37.5 on the injection pen. I screwed on a needle head, pinched the right side of my stomach fat, stuck, and released. *How exhilarating!* Well, actually it was extremely anti-climactic. I think I may have built it up a little more than I needed, but hey, it was a start and we were moving forward. I cleaned up the little bit of blood, got a sympathy kiss from my husband, placed the needle in my handy little "sharps" container—I was so excited when Cheryl gave this to me—and put the medicine back in the refrigerator for tomorrow night.

4

uninvited

After a few days of Cheryl monitoring me, the doctor *slowly* increased my dosage. My appointments became more regular—a couple of times in a week's span. We did more blood work and more ultrasounds. The routine was becoming as monotonous as brushing my teeth or combing my hair. But my follicles were starting to grow. I loved monitoring their progress in the mornings before I would head to work.

Excitement filled the cold, dark room as Cheryl continued to shove the wand-shaped transducer tool all around the inside of me. I usually just referred to the tool as the camera stick; it was much easier. She looked on my right side but didn't see many large follicles. Her words were nothing short of discouraging, but she knew as well as I did that it only took one follicle. I braced myself because now the camera stick was headed to my left side. She searched around for a while, and at the very last minute she saw one large follicle. This one was measuring at a 14! I didn't know *medically* what that meant, but *non-medically* speaking it meant *whooohoo*! This was large, and this one was going to work. That was the start of my little baby in there—I could already feel it.

Needless to say, that follicle wasn't quite strong enough. Just another negative pregnancy test at the end of my cycle was all the strength it had. I knew it was only the first cycle with our fertility team, but my hopes had been so high. A successful pregnancy was all starting to feel rather hopeless now. Zach and I tried all the time—every other day, to be exact. But it was causing tension between us. I felt sad. I felt frustrated. I felt angry. I felt every emotion except happiness. I didn't want to go out with our friends because I didn't want to fake any more smiles.

I'm so over it. I can't keep pretending!

Church is especially difficult right now. Every song we sing seems to make me cry. I feel like everyone is watching me—I know they aren't, but it feels like they are. I wonder what people are saying behind my back. I hate being invited over to places where I know there will be kids because I'm the only one without any. People include me in conversations, but I know it's just a pity inclusion. I go to parties and even though I'm physically involved in the conversations, mentally I'm just an outcast. I'm alone, looking in on everyone else and seeing the moms talk with other moms about mom things. They laugh about milestones and discuss upcoming birthday parties.

Uninvited!

I'm attending a party that I'm uninvited to; that's exactly how it feels. I don't belong here. I want to leave right now. I feel imprisoned in my own body, like there are bars surrounding me and all I want is to be released from this prison of pain. I get in the car after we stay the appropriate amount of time and burst into tears. Sometimes silent tears and sometimes full-blown sobbing tears. Life is miserable. Life is hopeless. I don't want to give up, but I sure question what the point is in all this. What lesson are you trying to teach me, God? Just make me understand faster! Please! I'm now at the point of begging. Give me a child. Fill my womb!

We were wrapping up teaching a series to the youth group on social media. I figured that would be a safe "no tears" series; I was wrong. One night, the video presenter talked about how social media only shows the *best* of peoples' lives. All the good is elevated, and the bad seems nonexistent. The rest of the lesson was hazy at best, but I remember being especially challenged that evening as I listened. Social media had been a real struggle for me lately. Everyone was sharing pregnancy announcements or posting about their kids and it made me sick to my stomach. I felt like a terrible person for not being able to control my emotions, but I was so envious and found myself just wanting what everyone around me seemed to have. I would "like" a post or a picture and then cry as I continued scrolling. Sometimes I would leave a congratulations comment and feel such bitterness as I hit the send button.

That night I remember making a conscious decision to get off of social media for a while. Why would I purposely place something in my path that only filled me with anger and resentment? Social media was only a stumbling block that brought no gain, no joy, and certainly no contentment.

5

I'm Never Adopting

⬩

hese feelings won't go away.[1] *I can't shake them. I refuse to think of becoming a mom in any other way than growing a huge stomach, going into labor in a hospital bed, and squeezing Zach's hand in excruciating pain. All the other women around me have had this opportunity. Some have even become pregnant without trying, and quite frankly, I'd go as far as to say, not planning either. I'm begging over here for a full womb, and all that shows up is emptiness.*

Emptiness!

Adoption is something I promise you I'll never do!

Never!

My mind immediately recalled part of a sermon I heard as a little girl: never tell God what you're not going to do because, sure enough, that's where you'll end up.

---

[1]   I strongly considered leaving this chapter out, but realized the importance of full transparency. After July 7, 2016, I can honestly say these thoughts never crossed my mind again. But before that day, they were a strong part of my heart and thought process and a very real and raw part of my journey. My sweet, firstborn, you are sitting on my lap as I write this. Your tiny little foot is pushing on my laptop screen and you keep looking up at me with your beautiful, big, brown eyes. I love you more than you will ever know and I'm so grateful that God changed my heart toward adoption and that you, my sweet boy, changed my life in the best way possible. I love you!

Well, fine! I won't technically say the words out loud, but I can guarantee you, I'm never adopting. It's a nice idea and good for all those people who do it, but not for me. I don't even know why I dislike the idea so much. I guess I just feel like it's not the real thing. It's a good second-best option, but it's more for people who have given up and really have no hope left. That can't be me. That's not the plan I have for my life. I'm a planner. That's what I do. Adoption hadn't even been on my radar until more recently, and now I just wanted it to go away. I refused to give up. I wasn't a quitter. We were working with a wonderful, trained medical staff who had success story after success story. We had every reason to believe a successful, natural pregnancy was right around the corner.

Lately, I've been afraid adoption is what God is going to make me do. I told Zach last night. He doesn't understand why I think it's such a terrible idea. He says we shouldn't give up trying yet either, but he actually likes the idea of adoption. If he does, he married the wrong girl. I can't adopt. I seriously can't. I'm not the right person for the job. Please, God, don't call me to this. I can't get it out of my head. I'm trying to go to sleep but all I think about is adopting. Stop crowding my thoughts. Just let me sleep!

Little did I realize, it was at this time small seeds of adoption were beginning to sprout in my heart and thoughts.

Please, God, just make me pregnant. You are an all-powerful God. You created the earth out of nothing. Making me pregnant would be so easy for you. I've waited a long time now. I've prayed; I've been in Your Word; I'm really trying. All I want is to grow our family. I'm not asking for anything bad. I promise You can use our child in any way You choose. If that means taking him to be a missionary to an unreached land when he grows, I'm fine with that. I give my baby to You; use him however You choose, just let me have a baby to give You. And let that baby come from me.

6
War Room

My mind drifted back to a few months before when we had visited Zach's family in Florida. It was New Year's Eve, and his family's church was showing the new movie *War Room*. If I'm being honest, I wasn't really expecting much from the film. I had seen some Christian films in the past and they seemed a little cheesy to me, so I figured this film wouldn't be much different. Little did I know the significance this film would soon have in my life. After the movie, we made plans with Zach's family to go downtown to watch the fireworks. I was sure that at least that part of the evening would be fun.

As the movie played, I almost tuned out. The movie was about a husband and a wife with a failing marriage. I couldn't relate to that plot line. I loved my husband very much. I would never cheat on him, and I had full confidence in his faithful love towards me. This whole infertility journey was hard, but never so hard that we got to the point of giving up on each other. In fact, lately I started seeing my husband in a whole new light. He was so understanding—even when he didn't understand. He held me when I cried and he prayed for me diligently. Our marriage wasn't headed down a path of ruins. Our marriage was growing. Nothing about this movie was relatable to me. *I'll keep watching though because, well, what else am I going to do: walk out?*

About halfway through the film, the idea came to me: a war room! That's it! I could make my own war room. For those who haven't seen the movie, I'll try to explain without giving away any spoilers. The woman in the film created her own war room, or prayer room, in her bedroom closet. She filled the wall with scriptures and prayers and spent time alone with God in the midst of all her life's trials. The war room became a place where she could go to be alone with God and cry out to Him for *His* answers for her life.

Where can I set up my war room? I couldn't have put one in our bedroom closet; it wasn't really set up for that. I could maybe have set one up in one of the closets in the spare bedrooms, but I wanted it to be private. What would happen when guests came to visit? I kept thinking. *What about our downstairs coat closet?* Behind the coat closet was a tiny space where the hot water heater was stored. *I'll check when I get home.*

When Zach and I returned from vacation, I thought I would explore my options. I went downstairs and entered the small, cramped space behind the coat closet. I was greeted with cobwebs surrounding every square inch of the hot water heater. Dead bugs, dirt and dust covered the ground—just as I had suspected. I got a tape measure and measured the actual sitting space— 4ft x 4 ½ ft x 3ft. *It's nothing but a cold, dusty, cement slab, but I think it might just be the perfect spot!* I got a wet cloth and began scrubbing. The floor was starting to look halfway decent, but it was quite cold and extremely uncomfortable. Then I remembered I had Zach's old college comforter stored away in a tote; that would make a perfect soft surface to sit on. I would need my Bible, a couple of pens, a notebook, and some tape so I could start decorating the walls.

I had been using my war room for a couple of weeks when one Monday afternoon I got home from work before Zach. I crouched down low and crawled behind the closet to sit down and start working.

I knew I had the house to myself for a while and dinner had minimal prep work that night, so I figured I would be good in there for a bit. As I was writing out my next verse on paper, I heard the key turn our lock and I realized Zach was already home from work. Normally, he was greeted with me standing in the kitchen working on supper or relaxing on the couch after my day of teaching, and when he didn't see me, he started calling out my name. I tried to escape my room before he noticed, but just as I was crawling out, my eyes were level with his shins.

"What are you doing down there?" he laughed, puzzled.

Busted!

A few weeks had passed since Zach first found me in my war room. One Saturday morning, I woke up only to realize Zach wasn't beside me in bed. This was highly unusual. Normally, we both enjoyed sleeping in on a Saturday morning. I checked the rest of the upstairs and didn't see him, so I walked downstairs. I didn't notice any lights on. *Where did he go? Wait!* As I looked a little closer, I noticed a small, dim light *was* on. A single light in the back of our downstairs coat closet, in the tiny space where our hot water heater was stored. He was using my war room.

For a while, this room saw the two of us on different occasions. One day, I remember looking at my wall where I had taped verses, prayers, lyrics, and prayer requests. I had a list of dates marking the first day we started trying to get pregnant and then marking every doctor's visit in between. Earlier in my journey, I found *31 Days of Prayer for Infertility* on some Pinterest website, so I wrote that out and taped it to the wall too. I would mark off each time I went through it, and cycle back to the beginning after the 31 days. There was a lot on this wall, but something was still missing.

I ripped out a piece of notebook paper and wrote, "Can I paint the word 'faith' on the wall?" Under the question I drew two boxes, one labeled "Yes" and the other labeled "No." I knew Zach would be in there again, and I wanted to see if he got my message. When I entered the room a couple of days later, the "Yes" box had a big check mark in it! I grabbed my paintbrush, a paper plate to hold the paint, and the only paint I had lying around the house—grey, boring old grey. From that day on, I loved walking into that room and seeing FAITH in huge letters plastered on the wall.

7

I Can't Help Crying

◇

Medicated cycle number two: here we go again. I still didn't like the Metformin pills, but I figured out that when I ate enough with them, my stomach didn't hurt near as much. I was still in the bathroom a lot though. I never knew when it was going to come on. I had absolutely no warning whatsoever. But, when it did come on, I didn't have much time before I needed to see a toilet—pronto! *Gross, but right now, that's life: gross, annoying, and painful. I don't care though. If this is what it takes to get a baby inside me, I'll commit to it for the rest of my life.*

Cheryl had been telling me for several days that my follicles were looking excellent; a couple in particular were growing large. *Time to up my shot dosage!* I got so excited when I received a call from the nurse in the afternoon telling me the doctor had looked over my morning's blood work and ultrasound, and had prescribed a higher dosage for the night. The actual phone call itself never lasted longer than a minute or two, but I clung to those phone calls and they made my day.

A few more days passed, and Cheryl was now even more surprised than she was a couple days before. The same follicles were still growing, and she was starting to prepare me for the possibility of not just one, but *two* babies. *What?!* Excited didn't begin to describe the emotions I was feeling. This was exactly what I had been hoping for

27

when we agreed to sign on with the fertility specialists. I was going to be a mom of twins! Zach and I were both shocked. That whole day I imagined two of everything. Two sets of eyes to stare back into mine, two beautiful mouths to give Mommy lots of smiles, and double the love. Yes, I also knew twins meant double the cries, double the messes, and double the diaper changes, but when you had waited as long as I had, everything else paled in comparison. *Twins! Can you believe it?!*

If I have to hear one more person complain about getting fat because she's pregnant, I'm going to scream. I have literally prayed for the exact thing they are complaining about. They seem so consumed with the inconvenience of the added baby weight wreaking havoc on their schedules and perfect physique, while I'm over here checking my stomach on a daily basis hoping for a few added pounds of baby fat.

For someone who has not experienced any difficulty in the world of conceiving, this phenomenon may seem a bit odd, but it's true. I prayed to gain an enormous, pregnant belly, and at the end of my cycles I prayed to wake up in the morning vomiting. I prayed all these things because the pain of not having a child far outweighed, in my mind, the physical pain of carrying one.

The ends of my cycles were the most difficult times. When it became clear that I wasn't pregnant, I would lose it. No matter how many times I tried to hold it together and not cry, it never worked. Lately, I had been trying to hide it from Zach. I hated him having to see me so sad all the time. All this infertility stress was taking a toll on him too. *He says he doesn't know how to help me, but he helps me more than he realizes.*

Part of the reason the ends of my cycles were so hard was because they were so inconsistent. Some months I would have a seemingly normal 30-day cycle, while other months I could go as long as 49 days in between periods. Talk about torture! Waiting that many days planted the pregnancy thoughts in my head that much more. Sometimes I would think I was pregnant several times in a month's span because of how long my cycles were lasting. I bought pregnancy and ovulation tests in bulk and had them shipped straight to my doorstep. Thank you, Amazon!

I can't help crying. The last time I realized another month was wasted and it was time to start back at square one was early on a Saturday morning. I went downstairs to my war room to cry so Zach wouldn't see me. I cried and prayed a lot that morning. When I went back upstairs, I thought I had it all together, but he knew. He opened his arms to hug me and then I lost it all over again.

Part Two: Reaping with Shouts of Joy

*For this child I prayed, and the LORD has granted me
my petition that I made to him.*

(1 Samuel 1:27)

8

Last Chance Month

The date was July 7, 2016. I was driving, yet again, to another doctor's appointment. We were now on cycle number three of our intrauterine insemination (IUI) treatments with our fertility specialist, and—needless to say—cycle two did not bring us the positive pregnancy test we were hoping for. This was our "last chance" month. If this month didn't result in a positive pregnancy test, we had to start looking at other options because we were only advised to try the IUI treatment for three cycles. Our next step would most likely be In Vitro Fertilization (IVF).

Normally, on my morning drives, I kept the radio off and I spent my time praying out loud to God. Jenny, a lady from our church, led a Sunday School lesson for the women a few months prior, and she said she often prays out loud so she doesn't get distracted by the busyness that life can bring. I began praying out loud on my drives to school, and it really did work. My prayers were much more meaningful and focused when I prayed out loud rather than praying silently with my mind wandering in a million different directions. When I started going to all the doctors' appointments, I decided to take her advice once again—with the exception of this particular morning. The radio was already turned on to HIS Radio when I got in the car, and I felt like singing mindlessly on my drive that morning. Unfortunately, at that point in the broadcast, there wasn't any music, but instead only talking. This was usually the time I channel-surfed. I love music, but get bored easily listening to commercials or people talking. I decided to leave the station where it was; it wasn't worth the effort to change the channel this morning.

The hosts of the show were interviewing a couple named Jennifer and Anthony Giugliano. Anthony shared that he had gone on a mission trip to Africa, and when he returned home, he told his wife their next step as a family was to adopt and bring their son home from Africa. They later shared how they made a Facebook post trying to sell Jennifer's wedding ring in order to help pay for the adoption costs of their son. She claimed that her diamond, a worldly possession, was worth nothing in comparison to the life of her child living halfway around the world.[2]

Tears began streaming down my face as I continued listening. I couldn't control myself. I would wipe them away, but another batch would pour out instantly. My heart was pounding out of my chest like it was about to explode. My hands became clammy as I continued to grip the steering wheel. I was nervous—not a scared nervous, but an excited nervous like I've never felt before. I had been blinded for so long and now it was as if God was giving me new eyes to see everything I once refused. Adoption was beautiful. Adoption was a treasured gift. Adoption was my calling.

I'm adopting!

In that moment it was so clear to me that this was God's plan for my life, and now I just needed to talk to Zach.

---

[2]   If you go to https://www.hisradio.com/home/greenville/, search "July 7," scroll down to "Highlights from Thursday, July 7, 2016," and click on "INTERVIEW: Anthony and Jennifer Talk About Adoption," you can listen to the 6 minute 55 second clip that God used to completely break my heart in the most life-changing way.

Looking back, it's so neat to see how God orchestrated my thinking and decision-making that morning. Such seemingly small decisions, but what a weight they would soon carry. *Thank you, God, for keeping my hands on the wheel and tuning my ears to hear Your voice.*

I pulled into the parking lot for my doctor's appointment. I was a mess! Mascara was running down my cheeks, my eyes were red, and I looked like a sad attempt of a woman. I grabbed the old napkins shoved in our glove box and tried to somehow make myself presentable. I walked in the door and Cheryl greeted me with the usual big hug and smile she always had. She drew my blood, and I lay down on the table for my ultrasound. The previous visits had been going well so far this month, and as I lay on the table today it only looked better. My follicles were growing in size which meant a high likelihood that at least one egg would be produced and released for fertilization. I watched her type the numbers into the computer. Not just one large one, but again, a couple of very large ones. Multiples were an even likelier possibility than last time, and even if it wasn't twins, surely one of those follicles would fertilize, and I'd be looking at a positive pregnancy test in the next week or so.

It's hard to explain how I was feeling in that moment lying on that table. This should have been an exciting appointment, but all I felt was complete indifference. I wasn't sad, but I wasn't excited either. I already knew it wasn't going to work, not because I was being a pessimist or losing faith, but because I *knew* that biologically giving birth wasn't how I was going to receive the title *Mom*. Honestly, I didn't even really want to go into that appointment after I heard the testimony on the radio station. For so long, my hope had been in specialists and medications, and now I was beginning to remember the words to the old hymn: "My hope is built on nothing less than Jesus' blood and righteousness. I dare not trust the sweetest frame, but wholly lean on Jesus' name."

Oh Lord, forgive me for placing all my hope in the people and things of this world.

That day felt like the longest day of my life as I waited to get home and tell Zach everything I was feeling. When we were finally both home from our long day of work, I told Zach I needed to talk to him about something. We both sat down on our couch, and I said I wanted him to listen to something. As I snuggled my head on his chest, his arm wrapped around me, I played the same testimony I heard on the radio station that morning. After he listened to it, I tried to tell him the change God had done in my heart, but I was doing more crying than speaking. In that moment, through our tears and a very long embrace, we both agreed that adoption was the next step in our journey to parenthood.

I've tried to put myself back in that moment to accurately describe how I felt. The only thing I can compare it to is the feeling of losing 100+ pounds of emotional baggage; it was like the weight of all the sorrow that had been building up for so long just fell off me instantly.

Instantly!

For 556 days I had put my hope in all the wrong places. I refused to consider adoption. I wanted my *own* pregnancy and I wanted it on my *own* time, and when none of that happened, there was nothing left but the feeling of hopelessness. Now, on day 557, instead of tears of hopelessness, I was crying tears of hope and excitement. I was in total awe and gratitude that God would choose this beautiful journey for us. I did nothing to deserve it, but by God's grace, He allowed me to see past myself and see the beauty that adoption would soon bring to our family.

Thank you, God, for being patient with me while I laid aside my pride and selfishness and am now beginning to open my heart to this new adventure.

9

I Will Come to You

After trying to conceive naturally, God had now given us a clear understanding of what He had called us to, but I had no idea where to turn for more information. Adoption was so foreign to me. No one in my immediate family had any experience with adoption, I didn't know of any friends currently going through the process, and I had no idea what my next step should be.

I was reminded of a girl named Heather Riley, (a friend of a friend of a friend—yes, you read that correctly—three friends removed). I asked for her contact information and figured it was my best shot to reach out to her. I emailed Heather that night and heard back from her right away. You know how sometimes there are people you encounter in life and, without ever meeting them, you can just tell they are a sweet, kind soul? I have met two on this journey and Heather was one of them. Our first email interaction began a series of emails back and forth. I asked her for advice and tips, and she fed me the words of wisdom I needed at the perfect time.

After calling a few local and national adoption agencies, Zach and I decided on one. This specific agency was the same one Heather and her husband were working with at the time. I found a great deal of comfort in knowing someone who was just a few steps ahead of us with the same agency. I called a couple of other agencies, but most had a month or so wait time before their next orientation. A couple of months doesn't seem like a long time in the grand scheme of things, but once I finally opened my heart to adoption, I was all in and was working faster than a speeding bullet every step of the way. On July 14, exactly one week after hearing the radio broadcast, we made our first contact with our agency and sent in our initial application, along with the first of many checks.

Our agency told us we would have to come to their home office for an orientation upon approval of our submitted application. That coming weekend was available for us, so I asked if we could come in the next couple of days. Unfortunately, I was a bit premature in my thinking. The earliest they could see us was August 4, 2016. That date seemed like an eternity's wait, but in reality, it was only a few weeks away—shorter than any of the other agencies I had contacted. I agreed to the earliest time they had available and began the countdown. In that time of waiting, we were so eager to share our news since, up until that point, the majority of our family and friends still didn't even know about our struggle with infertility.

We decided to start sharing the news with our families and began by calling each of our parents. Tears of joy and excitement became the overwhelming response. It felt so great to finally share the news we had kept a secret for so long. After all the conversations were over, we decided we also wanted to share our news with all our friends and extended family members, but how? We decided to write a letter. We first mailed it to our grandparents, aunts and uncles so they could hear the news of our adoption before the rest of the Facebook world. Here are some excerpts from the letter we posted to Facebook on July 26, 2016:

> Our relationship began as "love at first sight." We
> were college sweethearts and got married the summer

after we graduated. We both felt strongly that children would be part of our future. December 28, 2014, came, and we decided it was time to start expanding our family. One month turned into several months and not a single one went by without tears and heartache like I have never experienced. With each month that passed, negative pregnancy tests were all we were left with.

There came a point in March of 2016 that my normal OB/GYN could no longer do anything for us, and we were referred to a fertility specialist. Through all this, God has shown Himself faithful. We believed if God could speak the world into being, there was no doubt in our mind that He could give us a child. My greatest fear was how long I would continue to hear the answer I dreaded: *wait*.

Recently, God has been working in our hearts, and we both feel God calling us to pursue adoption! I can now say and <u>believe</u> without any hesitation to *"Count it ALL joy... when you meet trials of various kinds"* (James 1:2). I am grateful for the path God has chosen for us. Even through the darkest part of my life, God used it to point me to Himself. If you had asked me 564—and counting—days ago, I would have had a completely different response. Until now, my selfish heart couldn't see past my desire to have children biologically and stubbornly refused any other way. How wrong I was; biological or not makes no difference. This child will be OUR child—handpicked from God. What a special gift!

Through this journey, God has grown us individually in a special way, but also together. We have shed many tears of sorrow, but lately, so many more tears of JOY. What a beautiful picture of the gospel! He chose *me*, Leeann, to be a daughter of His. He chose Zach to be a son of His. He chose us when we could do nothing to contribute. One day, we will be able to speak to our child the very words spoken by Jesus to His disciples in John 14:18: "*I will not leave you as orphans; I will come to you.*" God adopted us as His own, and we will be able to demonstrate in a very real, personal, and tangible way the transformative power of the gospel in action.

We both feel as though our hearts could explode with happiness and anticipation, and oh, the stories we could tell of countless ways God has shown His faithfulness. However, we will simply end by asking you for the one thing we will so desperately need during this journey: <u>PRAYER</u>! Pray for patience as we continue to hear that word: *wait!* We also ask that you begin praying for our birthmother. While we do not know who she is, God has known her and prepared her for this moment in His sovereignty. She is the one who will be carrying our child, and we would ask you pray for her as she chooses *life* for our baby.

Those who sow in tears shall reap with shouts of joy!
(Psalm 126:5)

Encouragement filled our hearts. We were flooded with innumerable comments from friends and family with promised prayers to accompany this new journey. We felt an amazing outpouring of support from countless people, and to say it boosted our spirits would be the understatement of the century.

10
Orientation Day

August 4, 2016: our orientation day had finally arrived, and Zach and I made the three-hour drive to where our agency was located. We parked the car and, of course, had to take a selfie before going in to document this exciting day. When we walked in, Juliette greeted us. She was so sweet and put us at ease from her first *hello*. As the three of us walked to the back conference room, my heart was racing. *What will she tell us? Will all my questions be answered?* When we entered the room there was a huge table, much like what you would see in a dining room of a home, with fancy chairs around it. Juliette sat at the head of the table, and Zach and I took two seats on one side. The first thing she handed us was a gigantic two-inch binder stuffed with information. *Wow!* It was like she could read my mind because the next sentence out of her mouth was, "Now, don't be intimidated."

She began going through each tab and explained the different tab dividers: "Welcome," "Education," "Home Study," "Profile and Website," "Meeting the Expectant Mom," "Hospital Stay," "Financing," and "Miscellaneous." I started crying about halfway through the meeting. For so long I had been waiting to be a mom, and I finally felt like it was going to happen. I didn't need to worry if I was going to get a positive pregnancy test. The answer was already positive! God was *positively* going to bless us with a child by way of adoption. The beauty and comfort in knowing that truth was overwhelmingly emotional in such a joyous way. We walked out of the meeting with our heads spinning, but ready to hit the ground running. I was determined to do everything I could to get our part of the paperwork completed as quickly as possible.

Looking back, I think I was probably a very annoying client for my agency. I was constantly sending emails making sure they had what they needed from us, making sure they received every attachment to every email I sent, and persistently trying to work ahead as often as I could. We probably gave them a good laugh in the office on several occasions.

The form we prayed over the most was our "Child Desired" form. This form was essentially a checklist of things we were willing to accept in our future child, from ethnic background to openness with birth family, from birth family background to prenatal environment. There were many questions in each section. We wanted to be as open as possible because we trusted God would bring us the child He wanted us to raise in our home. God makes no mistakes, and we did not want to limit His plans for us. We spent a lot of time in prayer over this form, researching different things but mostly seeking wisdom from God.

II

Our Song

Sundays were often very difficult days. Every song we sang in the worship service was somehow a reminder of our journey and God's faithfulness, and would often stir up many emotions. One Sunday was particularly memorable. Our worship leader led us in the song "Never Once" by Matt Redman.[3] This song had always been special to me and reminded me of the circumstances we were facing in the different seasons of our life, and today was one of the first times I could sing it without breaking into tears. I noticed as I was singing that I didn't hear Zach's voice. This wasn't too uncommon. Zach would be the first to admit that his gifts and talents would never give him the "Vocalist of the Year" award. Still, I could usually hear him singing along in his own melodic way. I looked up to see my husband, who for so long had been holding it all together for the two of us, with tears streaming down his face. Every time he would wipe them away, it seemed like double the amount would come again. As I held my husband's hand, I knew exactly what he was thinking. We had been through so much in the last couple of years, a lot of struggles, a lot of emotional scars, and a lot of pain. But never once were we alone. Our God was, and is, faithful in every aspect of our lives. One day, at

---

[3]   Jason Ingram, Matt Redman, and Tim Wanstall

the end of our journey, we would be standing on a symbolic mountaintop as we held our precious baby for the first time. What a day of
rejoicing that would be! "Never Once" soon became *our song* in our
adoption journey.

Our nights rapidly filled with mounds of paperwork. We would
come home from a full day of working, eat supper, and then chip away
at our long list of requirements. We broke up the routine by taking
walks around our neighborhood. One walk, however, will be one that
gets told over and over. On that particular evening, we took a left out
of our driveway and began walking along the sidewalk on what we
thought would be our usual, uneventful, leisurely walk. We didn't
make it more than five to ten houses down the street when a tiny,
yippy dog came running out the front door. Growing up, my dad and
I would call these types of dogs "rat dogs." Now, if that had been a cat,
I would have high-tailed it in the opposite direction—yes, I have an
odd phobia of cats—but since it was a poor excuse for a canine, I stood
my ground and didn't even flinch. Some of the dogs in our neighborhood had underground fences, and I figured that was the case with
this dog. Even if it did manage to contact me, the worst thing that
could happen is I would get licked to death, or so I thought. I kept
walking, and Zach and I continued with our conversation. Most likely
we were talking about what paperwork we would complete when we
got back to the house, or our anticipation of meeting birthparents,
or when we would get the call from our agency; that was what most
of our conversations revolved around lately. The dog's yipping got
higher pitched and his short, stumpy legs seemed to be carrying him
like a gazelle now. He was headed straight for me.

"OUCH!" I screamed as the dog jumped up to bite my leg about
halfway up my calf.

Zach continued walking, and I instinctively bent down and grabbed my leg.

"Zach, I need to go back home," I said.

At this point he was laughing and continued walking ahead of me. He thought I was joking. I looked down and showed him my leg. There were seven raised lines, and my skin had been punctured with blood coming out in four places. He couldn't believe what he saw. He immediately went into full-blown doctor mode. After we did a great speed walk back to our house, he brought me up to our bathroom, soaked and cleaned out my cuts, covered them in ointment and bandaged me up. Now the doctor façade was gone and what was left was a man who was *not* happy. This tiny rat dog was now the most gruesome, wild, disease-carrying wolf-dog in Zach's mind.

"I'm going back to that house to see if anyone is home. We need to find out if they have shot records on that dog, and if not, I'm calling animal control so we can make a report. Get ready to go to the hospital. I'll be right back," he told me as if he was a drill sergeant giving orders.

Not more than five minutes passed, and Zach was back huffing and puffing at our front door.

"What happened to you?" I asked, trying unsuccessfully not to laugh.

"That dog came running after me too! I'm not going near that thing by myself!"

I burst out laughing. This tiny dog was causing so much drama. We both got in the car and drove over to the house hoping the dog was locked inside by now, but no such luck! The dog came jumping up at our car door barking incessantly. A neighbor noticed we were parked in the driveway of a house that clearly wasn't ours. She asked if she could help and we explained the story. No one seemed to be home, so we left a note on the door—well, let's be honest, the neighbor left a note on the door. We were not getting out of the car! Zach called animal control to document the incident, and we were told it would be in our best interest to get a rabies shot since we couldn't reach the dog's owners. Of course, it was after hours, so the only place we could go was the emergency room. This was not how we intended to spend our Sunday evening, and a visit to the ER was not going to be cheap! We were already saving every penny for the adoption.

Fast forward a couple of months and several phone calls later: we received a call from the insurance company of the dog's owners offering us a $2,500 settlement to cover the cost of the emergency room and the inconvenience the situation caused. At first, I thought it was some kind of scam. I couldn't believe it. I was just hoping we would not have to pay the ER bill, but where was all this extra money coming from? This was just one of the awesome ways God chose to provide for us financially in our adoption process: a gift that was totally unexpected, but so much fun to deposit directly into our adoption account. To this day, anytime we want something extra for our home, or our car is in the shop and needs to be fixed, Zach jokes that I need to grease up my leg with some bacon fat and take a walk around the block.

12
Making Progress

In the back of my mind I kept thinking about the radio broadcast and how the Giugliano family and their testimony changed my life. If it wasn't for their story, would I still be driving to early morning doctor visits and placing my hope in all the wrong places? I wanted so badly to contact Jennifer Giugliano and share with her how much her story impacted my life for the better.

When I got home from work one day, I looked up an email address for HIS Radio. I emailed Allison Storm, the morning show co-host, and briefly shared our situation adding that I would love to share our story in more detail with Jennifer if I could have her contact information. I had little faith that my search would go any further than that. I figured the radio station probably received fan mail often, and mine would get lost in the shuffle. Exactly fifty-four minutes later, I got an email back saying how much joy they received upon opening my email and that Jennifer would love to hear from me. Her email address was attached. I quickly sat at my computer and started emailing this woman I had never met.

I mentioned earlier that there were two people I encountered on this journey who, without ever meeting them, held—and continue to hold—a very special place in my heart; Heather was the first, and

Jennifer was the second. My initial contact with Jennifer started a series of emails back and forth between the two of us. She began following our adoption page on Facebook, and we kept in touch regularly. Jennifer and her husband were still in the process of bringing their son home from Africa at the time. She was such an encouraging friend to me, and God placed her in my life at just the right time. We were both walking similar journeys, and we both lifted each other up in prayer. I am so thankful for her sweet spirit and friendship. I'm thankful for the courage she and her husband displayed by sharing their story publicly, and for the example they set—and continue to set—as followers of Christ. I believe God uses His people to help carry out His purpose in the lives of His children, and I believe God used Jennifer and her husband to prune my heart to see the beauty of adoption on that July morning.

August 20, 2016, was a successful day for all three of us: Zach, me, and our dog Sophie. Sophie went to the vet to get her vaccinations all up-to-date for our agency records, and Zach and I got fingerprinted. One hundred bucks for them to scan my hand on a computer screen— all of which took about ten minutes, tops—and tell me I'm not a criminal. I couldn't complain though; we were making progress. At that point, our paperwork was finally nearing an end. However, we were still working on completing our twelve hours of education credits. This wasn't as bad as it sounds. Basically, we had to read a total of two books and ten assigned adoption-related articles.

One of the books we chose for our required reading, *Adopted for Life* by Russell Moore, is an excellent book that I would highly recommend. Moore does a great job of combining practicality with the true heart of the gospel. We also had dates now for our home study visits: September 3 and September 10, at 9 a.m. *How exciting!*

While working on all our paperwork, I had also been working on creating our profile book for prospective birthmothers. We started off with a letter to the birthmother, and then we introduced ourselves with pictures and short explanations. We included a couple of baby pictures, a summary of how we met, our wedding, our families, and a lot more. The profile book would be the first impression for the birthmothers to decide if Zach and I were a good fit for their baby. I spent hours putting this book together and imagining what our birthmother would think as she flipped through the pages. As we wrote the *Dear Birthmother* letter together, I pictured our meeting her one day. I envisioned running up and giving her a big hug. As often as I prayed for our future child, I prayed for her too. I didn't know what life experiences she would be facing or what factors would play a part in her decision, but I knew it was probably one of the most difficult decisions she would ever make.

After endless hours of working on our profile book, it was finally complete. We were told to order ten copies originally, but since our agency was in the process of expanding and opening another location, they said to go ahead and order fourteen. All of these books would be distributed to the different agency locations across the United States. The final cost of the books after shipping was going to be around $630.00. I had been praying we would find a good deal, and the Lord specifically answered that prayer. God provided unexpected discounts that saved hundreds of dollars and I was able to purchase all fourteen books for only $253.62. I was so excited that I began sharing our story of provision with so many people. Seeing God answer our prayers even down to the tiny details was amazing. Matthew 6:26 says, "Look at the birds of the air: they neither sow nor reap nor gather into barns, and yet your heavenly Father feeds them. Are you not of more value than they?" I remember feeling that verse in a very personal way many times throughout our journey. All God wanted us to do was trust Him. He would take care of the rest.

13
A Tangible Reminder

September 3, 2016, was the day of our first home study visit with our social worker. I had been running around the house like a madwoman the previous few days cleaning every nook and cranny. I also baked some pumpkin chocolate chip muffins because our agency said it was a nice gesture to have food and drink available for the social worker. The Wednesday prior at church a couple of our friends left a beautiful bouquet of flowers with a note by our car. The note read:

> Zach and Leeann—
>   We are praying for your upcoming home visits.
> These flowers are a tangible reminder of the many
> prayers and support you have—and of course to add
> a little special touch and hospitality. We love you
> and are excited for you.
>
> > Much love,
> > John and Jessica

I couldn't wait to set the flowers on my kitchen table for our visit. To this day, I still have that note sitting in the very same vase in my china cabinet. I often catch a glimpse of it as I'm walking in and out of our dining room. The note reminds me of all the prayers that were prayed over our adoption journey. The outpouring of love and support we received from friends and family all over the globe always lifted our spirits and brought so much encouragement. I've never felt more in the center of God's will than when we set out to pursue adoption. It's hard to explain, but powerfully true. When I finally let go of my own plans and means to become a mother and let God truly direct my steps, I never once questioned our decision to adopt. I continually felt God's hand even in the most mundane parts of our check-off list for our agency, and I was filled with an overwhelming joy at the thought of growing our family in this way.

Ding-dong, ding-dong. I heard the doorbell ring. Actually, I already knew the social worker was there because for the last half hour I had been gawking through our blinds checking for her arrival.

Don't open the door yet, Leeann. You don't want her to know you've been watching her through the peephole since she pulled up by the mailbox.

After the appropriate amount of time passed, we opened the door and welcomed her into our home. Kim seemed very nice. I offered her a seat at our table—everything I had read said that you should have a hard surface for them to write on—but she said she felt more comfortable on the couch. *I wasn't planning on her sitting on my couch. Of course she's wearing black leggings and my dog sheds her yellow-lab coat like it's her job. Hey, Kim, there is a lot less hair on the wooden kitchen chairs—and she's sitting on the couch. Great!*

I offered her a homemade, pumpkin chocolate chip muffin and a drink, but she politely refused. *Am I coming off too strong? Maybe I offered too much at one time? Maybe it's the pumpkin. I love pumpkin, but not everyone does. I should have gone with the blueberry.*

As it turned out, the couch was a much better choice anyway. We all sat down in the living room and it was a very relaxed setting. She asked some questions about our family values and our individual upbringings. Later, we gave her a tour of our home. I was very thankful for a husband who was able to think on the spot with well-articulated answers. I tended to freeze with some of the questions, but Zach spoke with eloquence and came through to save the day.

Our second home visit was a week later and mainly focused on our individual interviews. Kim sent Zach upstairs and began my interview first. The interview itself was all very laid back. She asked me questions as if she was just trying to get to know me better. I had to explain my family background, how Zach and I met, and why we were seeking adoption. She asked questions about how we divide the roles and responsibilities of our household, and how we would raise our future children. After she was finished with my interview, I went upstairs and Zach came downstairs to be interviewed. After both our individual interviews were completed, Kim had us sit down together and asked us a few more follow-up questions.

On September 14, 2016, all our paperwork was officially completed and turned in to our agency. All we had to do now was wait for our social worker to type up our official home study report. What a relief it was to not have anything left to check off our list. No more appointments to schedule or articles to read. No more questionnaires to complete, forms to be signed, or fingerprints to be scanned. We were done!

14
I Don't Even Know Her Name

What is an open adoption? I had no idea the answer to this question initially. Most of the agencies we looked at highly recommended at least a semi-open adoption and greatly discouraged closed adoptions. When we started considering this possibility, we immediately were faced with the "You don't want to do that; the baby's mom could come after the child" comments. While all well-intended, these comments were simply inaccurate.

Zach and I agreed that we would be open to sending our child's birthparents letters and pictures if that was something they wanted us to do. We also heard of people setting up a website for the adoptive parents and birthparents as an ongoing place to share photos and big events. We agreed that after we met the birthparents and were given more information, we would be open to the idea of exchanging phone numbers for occasional phone calls and texts. To some people this was very alarming and raised many red flags. We understood that not everyone would agree with our decisions, but none of our decisions were made without lots of prayer and research.

This woman was about to give us the greatest earthly gift we could ever imagine. How could we not share a photo now and then to show her she had made a good choice and that her baby was in safe and loving hands? That was our view on the matter. We knew we were required to have a finalization of the adoption in a courtroom before a judge, and, legally speaking, there was no way for someone to *come after our child* once that was completed. At that moment all paperwork, including a new birth certificate, would have our names listed as the child's parents. We also felt that some type of communication would allow us to be a testimony for Christ. Maybe our future child would be the means that God would choose to use to bring his birth family to the saving knowledge of Jesus Christ. We dared not remove that possible opportunity. Zach and I always had the mindset that God was in control and leading in every step of our journey, and He would work out every detail according to His perfect will.

Before walking the adoption path, I had a preconceived mindset that we would never know our child's birthparents and we would never have an open adoption. The more I learned, the more excited I was at the prospect of someday meeting our baby's birthparents. I couldn't wait for our first hug, and I couldn't wait to thank her like I've never thanked anyone in my life. I pictured us calling each other every now and then to catch up and texting her pictures of our baby as he grew older. My favorite moment to envision was her coming to visit our church one Sunday with us. Every time I envisioned that possibility, I would tear up.

Zach and I were both in agreement that our child would know as much about his birthparents as they were comfortable sharing. Adoption wouldn't be a secret in our home, but a story we would share often, remembering the glorious deeds of the Lord.

October 25, 2016, was a special day. At 10:25 that morning, we were officially considered a "waiting family" with our adoption agency. Being a waiting family meant our agency could begin showing our profile book to birthmothers. That was the good news. The bad news was that, according to our adoption agency, the expected one to three years of waiting could now officially *begin*. We did not let this discourage us. Instead, we saw the glass half full version of this news, and we were eagerly anticipating *the call*. I began thinking more and more about our birthmother. She was in my thoughts as much as our future child. A few days later, I wrote this post on our adoption Facebook page:

> *I may not know her name, but not a day goes by that I don't think of her. I wonder where she is, how she is, if she's going through this pregnancy with loved ones, or if she's all alone and scared. I wonder what her day looks like, what her favorite things are, if she's thinking of us as much as we think about her. I can't wait for the day when we meet her and I will finally be able to give her a long-awaited hug. I'm so thankful for the strength and the deep love she has for our baby in choosing to give life, even though it could quite possibly be the hardest thing she has ever had to do. She has a very special place in my heart already, and I don't even know her name.*

On November 4, I got a text from Juliette at our adoption agency. My hands started shaking. I began thinking, *Could this be it? Could this be the call already?* I called her back immediately only to find out there was a small hiccup in moving forward. All the profile books we ordered had our last name referenced throughout the book. This was a mistake that our agency—and we ourselves—had overlooked prior to ordering. Until we were officially matched with a birthmother, last names from either party had to be kept confidential, and even after a match was in place, a certain amount of privacy was highly encouraged to protect everyone involved. The good news was that we would be reimbursed for the new order; the bad news was that now we would have to wait even longer to have our book shown to potential birthmothers. I was so disappointed. I tried to stay positive about the situation, but this was certainly a hard pill to swallow.

That night when I got home from work, I went straight to our computer to delete our last name from every page where it appeared. I did a quick double-check and then ordered fourteen more copies to be sent directly to our agency. I took a breath and realized that five to ten business days for shipping wasn't going to be the end of the world, and it would all work out in God's timing, according to His perfect will.

15
Stay by Your Phone

⬨

It was Thursday, November 10—only six days after I placed the new order of profile books. I woke up at my normal 6 a.m. wake-up time, hooked our dog, Sophie, outside to eat and relieve herself, and walked back upstairs to get ready for another day of teaching. I brushed my teeth, straightened my hair, and put on my makeup. Nothing was out of the ordinary. In fact, I'm very much a creature of habit, so this was the same routine I had been practicing for the past five years. I put on the outfit I had laid out the night before and walked back downstairs to pack my lunch and let Sophie back inside. When all my bags were packed, I ran back upstairs one last time to kiss Zach goodbye. I hated leaving each morning, especially lately. I would often think about how nice it would be to one day alter my routine to include messy diapers, making bottles, tripping over toys, and morning snuggles. I hopped in my car, backed out of my driveway and started my morning prayer time on my drive to work.

Dear God, I thank You for this day that You have provided. This is the day that You have made; let me rejoice and be glad in it. Thank You for the jobs You have provided Zach and me, and the home You have given us. Help me not to forget that the very breath I breathe is only because You choose to let me live another day. Lord, I pray today for Zach, that You would watch over him on the roads as he goes to and from work. I pray You would keep him safe and keep a hedge of protection over his car. I thank You for the man he is and the time he spends in Your Word. I pray You would continue to keep him close to You and not let him get distracted by the things of this world. I thank You for the love he shows me daily. Help me to be a better wife and continue to stay in Your Word. Lord, I pray now for our birthmother. I don't know where she is or what she is doing. I don't know if she is pregnant yet or not. I don't know if she's alone and keeping this a secret or if she has the support of family, but I pray You would watch over her and protect her. I pray You would be with our baby, keep him or her safe and keep Your hand of protection over our birthmother's growing body. I pray this child would come to know You at a very early age and have a desire to serve You faithfully. I pray that we would be patient as we continue to hear the word "wait," and I pray if it be Your will, we would meet our baby soon. Thank you for opening our hearts to adoption and for all the many blessings You have provided along the way. I pray that if our birthparents do not know You, that through our adoption we would be a testimony for You and that they may come to know You as their personal Savior. I pray You would be with me today as I go to school. I pray that I would not stress, but trust in You for my every need. Thank You for all You do daily for us. Amen!

My assistant was out for a doctor's appointment, so I had a substitute in my classroom all day. I had managed to make it to the afternoon with only one more class to go, and then the last period was my planning period. My students were working on a group project when I noticed I had a missed call and text from Juliette from our agency. It seemed weird to be hearing from her today. The text read:

(1:11 p.m.) Juliette: Hi Leeann. Can you give me a call when you get a chance? I wanted to run a situation by you with a baby born yesterday.

(1:13 p.m.) Me: Yes definitely!!:) My class gets over at 2:15 can I call then?

(1:31 p.m.) Juliette: Well I'll be showing your profile book then. Stay by your phone. Here's the info as I know it right now: A.A. boy born yesterday at 34 weeks; currently in the NICU.

I couldn't believe what I was reading. *Was this really happening?* We had only been officially "waiting parents" for 16 days. I wondered if she had even received the second shipment of our corrected profile books. I was really shaking now, and my heart was beating like never before. I didn't know what to do. The sub in my class was a favorite and very familiar with our group of kids, so I told her I needed to step out of the room for a second to make a quick phone call. I called Zach and somehow managed to relay the message I just received from Juliette and then almost immediately started crying. He said, "Go call her now. Don't wait. Call me right back."

Why didn't I just do that in the first place? I wasn't thinking clearly. I stood under the staircase in the school hallway and called Juliette. She sounded just as shocked as I felt. She couldn't believe this was happening either. She said there was a husband and wife and they just recently moved to the area. They didn't have an adoption plan prior to moving, but when they arrived at the hospital, they asked for a list of local adoption agencies. The list they were given was in alphabetical order, and there were other agencies listed above ours; it's only by God's grace they somehow decided to call our agency. Juliette told me she had three other books to share but they were all out-of-state couples and we were the only one in-state. I thought that was odd, but I didn't question it. She also told me that our books hadn't arrived before she left the office, so she took labeling tape and whiteout to our profile book and covered all the places our last name appeared.

I asked how the baby was doing. She said the baby was doing great and he was being taken care of by the nurses in the Neonatal Intensive Care Unit (NICU). The birthmother had no prenatal care, and everything about this scenario was very out of the ordinary. I remember she kept saying, "This never happens. This seriously never happens like this." Juliette told me the birthparents were very set on adoption and she didn't see them changing their mind. This was encouraging to hear, but my mind was still in a whirlwind. After we chatted a bit longer, she told me to start praying because she was about to show our profile book and she would call me back with whatever decision they made. We said our goodbyes and hung up.

Both our voices ended with such excitement and anticipation. I was nervous thinking of our next conversation, but in the back of my mind, I knew this was *our* baby I was praying for. I can't explain it. While part of me was desperately praying for them to choose us, another part of me already knew they would. I'm so thankful God allowed both of those powerful emotions to simultaneously intersect in my mind. The nervousness allowed me to still cling to God and remember that He was ultimately in control of the entire situation, and the feeling of certainty allowed my faith in God to rise to a whole new level. I immediately went back to my room. By that time my students had been dismissed and it was an empty, quiet classroom. I called Zach to share the news I got from Juliette. He immediately prayed with me on the phone. I loved that. I was crying through his prayer, but I could hear in his voice a sense of hesitant excitement, the kind of feeling I assumed he would have if I had ever had the chance to tell him I was pregnant for the first time. I used to plan out special ways to surprise him that he was going to be a dad. I remember having so much fun trying to work out every little detail in my imagination. Calling him on the phone when we were both in the middle of our workday was never one of those cute Pinterest ideas I had envisioned.

We decided we should let our parents and siblings know what was happening so they could be praying with us. Zach and I exchanged *I love you's*, he called his parents, and I called mine. Now, all that was left to do was *wait*. Waiting was something we should have been great at by now, but this was one of the hardest times of waiting I have ever experienced in my life.

I remember looking at my to-do list sitting beside my laptop, but not being able to cross off one single item. I watched the minutes pass on my cell phone clock waiting for her to call me back. *Has it happened yet? Did they go with someone else and she is calling that couple before she calls and breaks the news to me? What did they think when they looked at our book?* Questions ran through my mind like they were competing for first place in a race. Eventually, the bell rang and afternoon announcements began echoing over the speakers. The minutes continued to pass, and by this time it had been about two hours since I had talked to Juliette. All of a sudden, my phone rang.

"Hello?" I answered, waiting to hear the tone of Juliette's voice on the other end.

"They picked you. They chose your book first and didn't even look at the others. They said you both were the perfect fit."

I couldn't believe what I was hearing, yet at the same time, I was not surprised at all. I don't remember much more of our conversation, probably because all I kept hearing was, *they picked you.* Juliette said the birthparents would not be officially allowed to sign over consents until 9 o'clock the next morning, but she told us to plan to make the drive tonight so we were at least in the same zip code and would be able to meet our son the next day.

Our.

Son.

After we hung up, I began racing around my room trying to get as much organized as possible, not knowing when I would return to teaching. After I managed to piece together some order of lesson plans, I went to share the news with my principal. At that point, only one of my teacher friends knew and was frantically helping me try to organize the chaos. We shared a joyful and tearful hug goodbye, and I raced out the door of the school building and called Zach as I was driving home. I've never heard my husband's speech so discombobulated, "I'll drive home now. Should I stay at work until you get home? No, I'm leaving now. I'll start packing when I get home."

He was much closer to home than I was, so he had me beat by a good twenty minutes or so. When I got home, we embraced and then ran around the house still trying to wrap our heads around the last few hours. Normally, when we go on family vacations, I'm the one who packs for both of us. I knew Zach was so proud of himself because when I got home, he said he laid all his stuff out in a pile for me to throw in the suitcase. I went upstairs to find his pile ready to be packed: a bottle of contact solution, dress shoes, a belt and a pair of gym shorts. Laughter poured from my mouth and my heart was bursting with joy. My husband just found out he was going to be a daddy. I just found out I was going to be a mommy. Oh, and did I mention we had nothing for a baby except one Rock 'n Play Sleeper I picked up at a yard sale, and a hand-me-down Pack 'n Play our friends had given us? I knew God was about to provide in some big ways, and I could not wait to see how.

16

Jehovah Has Heard

fter our bags were packed and we were in the car, I called my
aunt and uncle who lived near the hospital to let them know we
would be intruding houseguests for the next few days. They couldn't
believe what they were hearing, and they reciprocated all our excitement.

As we were driving, our emotions started to take control even
more. We would be laughing and then break into tears almost simultaneously. I've heard people refer to their emotions as a roller coaster
ride, and, at the risk of sounding cliché, that's exactly how I would
explain our three-hour drive to my aunt and uncle's house. In the
midst of all our tears and laughter, we realized we hadn't picked out
a name. I started Googling names as Zach drove. Some names Zach
liked and I didn't, and others I liked and Zach didn't. Not long into the
drive we came across the name Jayden. Jayden means *thankful* and the
name also derives from the Hebrew name Jadon meaning, "Jehovah
has heard." We both instantly fell in love with this name. We knew
his birthparents had named him Jonas and we wanted to keep that as
part of his name also, so we decided on Jayden Jonas Hale. Now we
had the name and we couldn't wait to see the face that would soon
hold that name.

Juliette called us as we were driving to give us more specific instructions for the next day. She told us the signing of the paperwork shouldn't take too long, and following that, she would meet us in the lobby of the NICU. I asked her if there was a chance the birthmother would want to meet us, but she said she didn't think so. I told her I understood, but to at least let her know that Zach and I were open to the possibility if she changed her mind. I began praying she would. I longed to meet her and I prayed this prayer multiple times.

Neither of us slept at all that night. Maybe it was because we were snuggled on my cousin's twin-sized bed, but I think in this case, it was more of the nervous anticipation of what would soon come our way. Our minds were racing, and we couldn't wait to get to the hospital the next morning. Technically speaking, Jayden wasn't *ours* yet, not until the paperwork was signed, and that wouldn't happen until 9 o'clock the following morning. There was still a chance that this would all fall through, and trying to find a balance between two polar opposite emotions was not an easy feat. I lay awake wondering if I could afford to quit my job and stay home—which was the plan after the school year was over. My income for the 2016-2017 school year was how we had planned to cover our adoption bills. I thought about our birthmother and wondered if I would see her tomorrow. I tried to picture holding our son for the first time. I hated knowing that he was all alone, and I wished so badly I could be with him. Millions of other thoughts raced through my mind, and finally I realized it was morning.

17
My Name and Heart Forever Changed

*T*oday is the day I will meet my son!

My.

Son.

When I got dressed, I was careful not to spray any perfume. I wanted Jayden to smell *my* scent as I held him close on my chest. We quickly got dressed, grabbed the snacks my aunt packed for us, and hit the road for the twenty-minute drive to the hospital. We arrived at 8:45 a.m. and headed straight for the waiting room where Juliette had told us to meet her. We started off by sitting but soon became very anxious. Zach began pacing the small waiting area back and forth.

(9:08 a.m.) Juliette: Mom is signing consents now
(9:09 a.m.) Me: Wow! Wonderful!!!

Tears just flowed from our eyes. Zach grabbed my hand and said, "Let's pray." By that time both of us needed to use the restroom with all our nervous energy, but figured Juliette would be coming to get us any minute. The more time that passed, the more fearful we became that something was going wrong. *Did they change their minds? Were they having second thoughts?*

(10:03 a.m.) Juliette: We're waiting on dad now
(10:03 a.m.) Juliette: We're halfway home:)
(10:03 a.m.) Me: Wow, you weren't kidding when you said they had a lot to sign. :)

Still waiting. Zach continued pacing and we both kept sending up prayers on our own. *What on earth is taking so long?*

(10:35 a.m.) Juliette: Yes, there's a great deal of information. ... Just hang in there for me. This should be wrapped up within a half hour. There is coffee and food downstairs if you want them :)
(10:36 a.m.) Me: Haha, thanks:) our nervous excited stomachs can't handle that right now I don't think:)
(10:39 a.m.) Juliette: As soon as he signs and we wrap up, I will come find you. When you stepped off the elevator on the 6th floor, which direction did you go?
(10:40 a.m.) Me: Left, we're like 15 ft from elevator. The waiting room says, "OB triage"

We were faced with another long pause and more waiting. Almost another hour had passed. I kept checking my phone every few seconds to make sure I didn't miss anything. We were starting to get texts from our parents checking to see if it was official yet.

(11:30 a.m.) Juliette: Coming to get you now :)
(11:31 a.m.) Me: Whoohoo!!!!

At that point we still weren't one hundred percent sure how everything went. I assumed from her smiley face in the text that it was good news, but I had to hear it from her in person to truly believe it was happening. We both stood up—like standing up was going to make it happen any faster—and started looking out for her. The only time we had met her was three months before for our initial orientation. *Would I recognize her? Would she recognize us?* And then I saw her. She was the lady walking towards us with a huge smile and tear-filled eyes. She sat us down and explained that all the paperwork had been signed, and if we were ready, we could go walk down to see our son.

Our.

Son.

If we were ready? *Yes!* We were most certainly ready. She later told me that the morning before she left for the hospital, the box of our corrected profile books had been delivered. We laughed at the irony the last few days had brought us.

We had to scrub up to our elbows, remove our rings and put our cell phones in a plastic bag. As we entered the darkened NICU, Juliette said she would be right behind us taking pictures. The nurse led the way into a curtain-closed section. As we walked in, my hand went immediately to cover my mouth in amazement. We looked in at our 5 lb 13 oz baby boy sleeping peacefully with cords attached all over his tiny body. The nurse said our timing was perfect since he was due for his next feeding. I sat in the chair and she handed me my son.

My.

Son.

My name and my heart were now changed forever. I was a *mom!* Until I saw him for the first time I never dreamed I could love anyone as much as I instantly loved this tiny boy. For so long I had waited for this moment, I had dreamed of this moment, and now my reality was better than anything I had previously envisioned. Just when I thought it couldn't get any more perfect, Jayden opened his mouth to yawn and gave us a glimpse of his beautiful eyes. I prayed, *"Thank*

You, Lord, for this tiny baby boy. Thank You for blessing us beyond what we could have asked or thought."

After a while, Juliette left, and our nurse said she would give us some time alone as a family. The first song we played for Jayden was "Never Once" as we held him and rocked him in our arms. We thought back to the Sunday weeks before when we sang that song in church and looked forward to this very moment in the hospital room. We wanted Jayden to know that God had been, and would continue to be, with us every step of the way in leading us together as a family. He was and is faithful over everything. To this day, that song is the one song that can make him go from full-blown alligator tears to the biggest smile you've ever seen within seconds of hearing the instrumental introduction.

As we sat in the room, we treasured the time we had to hold him before we had to put him back in his isolette. The nurses and doctors were monitoring his bilirubin levels, lung development, and his temperature. We were told he would need to stay in the NICU for approximately two to three weeks before being discharged to go home. We were blessed. We were joyful. We were *parents*.

18

Blessings

⬡

We began to receive blessings left and right. My aunt was telling our story to some of her friends while watching my cousin's basketball game, and they were so touched by God's blessing and timing for our family that they wanted to throw me a baby shower. Since we were told Jayden would be in the hospital for at least two to three weeks, they planned the shower for a little less than two weeks away. A few days later, while sitting with Jayden in the hospital, I was told by one of the nurses that he was making so much progress he would probably be out sooner than expected. As it turned out, Jayden was moved to the NICU 2—less intensive—in five days and discharged completely after only nine days. This meant the baby shower was going to need to be pushed up.

On November 17, a group of ladies—a handful that I knew and loved, but most of whom I had never even met—along with my aunt, threw me a beautiful shower. They had a theme with cake and napkins to match the meaning of Jayden's name—thankful—and presents galore. This first-time mom who had nothing at all for her newborn baby was now loaded with enough supplies for a set of twins. I received clothes, diapers, wipes, blankets, toys, medicine drawer essentials, money and much more. In fact, the lady who opened her home for the shower was finishing knitting Jayden's blanket as I was opening gifts. The amount of gifts I opened from people I had never met will forever fill my heart with gratitude. I felt so grateful sitting in that room surrounded by women who loved me and my baby in a way that I'll never quite be able to explain or understand. Little did I know, our church back home was busy planning a calendar of meals for us when we arrived home, and my school and church were planning baby showers for us as well. My God is a faithful provider! That has never been more clear to me than in our journey of adoption.

Zach arrived after the shower and we loaded up our vehicle with all our new treasured gifts. We went off to bed, excited for the next morning when we would be able to finally take our baby home.

When we arrived at the hospital the following morning, we couldn't wait to hold Jayden and get him dressed in his new clothes for our drive home. We rocked him and cuddled him until the doctor made his rounds and gave us the final clearance to head home. Just before we were ready to head downstairs, I received a call from a Medicaid worker in the hospital. She asked that we stop by her office on the first floor before we left. *What is this about?* I wondered. We had never qualified for any Medicaid services before, so I wasn't sure why anyone would be contacting us now. I figured it had something to do with Jayden, but I was still confused.

When we walked into her office, she told us she had been given our names and heard our story. *Wow! Word sure travels fast in these hospital halls!* I still had no idea what this all meant or why she asked to see us. Since Jayden was brought into our lives so quickly, I really didn't have time to think many things through. This quick visit to a stranger's office turned into one of our biggest blessings by far.

She explained that since Jayden's birthmother qualified for Medicaid at the time of her delivery, Jayden would also be covered by Medicaid for the first year of his life. At that point, I still didn't truly comprehend what that news meant for our family. It was only as the year went on that I was able to fully grasp and appreciate this amazing gift. Every doctor's visit Jayden had was completely free. All of his formula—including the specialty formula he was on for the first few months—and baby food were free. When he had to visit the ophthalmologist for his ptosis (drooping eyelid) and blocked tear duct, we didn't pay a dime. This was such a huge burden lifted after the large invoices we had to pay back to our agency at the time of Jayden's arrival. Also, because I took an extended maternity leave, my paychecks were now rather skimpy-looking, and we were originally relying on my full year's teaching salary to pay for this adoption. We exchanged phone numbers in her office and I thanked her for being so diligent in tracking us down. She knew we were in a hurry to get started on our three-hour drive home, and she said she would be in touch.

Zach pulled the car up as I stood with Jayden and the nurse on the side of the curb. My mind was still in a daze with everything that had happened over the past few days. I handed Zach the car seat, he clicked it into the base in the back seat of the car, and we were on the road. As Zach drove, my mind drifted back to just a week before when we were on the road headed in the opposite direction, with not a single item of baby clothing, no name for our son, and still wondering if his birthparents would change their minds at the last second. Now we were headed home, our car packed floor-to-ceiling—and every square inch in between—with our son sleeping peacefully in the backseat. I was blessed beyond words.

19

Joy Unspeakable

◇

T wenty-two hours and nineteen minutes was the amount of time we had to prepare to be parents. Most mothers can give a nine-month warning period to their spouse, but not this momma. Our days were now filled with spit-up, snuggles and diaper changes, and our once peaceful nights were interrupted with the cries of a small, helpless child. I wouldn't say everything was smooth sailing upon bringing our son home because that would be a lie. We weren't any different from any other couple bringing a baby into their lives. I didn't always greet Jayden with a soft lullaby when he woke up crying in the middle of the night. In fact, some nights I was so exhausted, I wanted to pretend I didn't hear his cries right next to my bed. There were days my husband would come home from a long day of work only to be welcomed with all my problems from the day. We weren't perfect parents just because we had wanted a child for so long, but we learned, and we grew, and we were abundantly grateful for God's beautiful blessing.

During my season of infertility, I remember praying Psalm 37:4: "Delight yourself in the Lord, and he will give you the desires of your heart." I wondered then why God didn't answer my request. I wasn't praying for anything bad; I was simply praying to be a mom. That verse left me with much confusion and many questions of why God seemed to be ignoring me. That same verse is now especially near and dear to my heart for the same reason it bothered me years ago. You see, during my season of infertility I wasn't completely delighting myself in the Lord. Sure, I prayed, I read my Bible, and I went to church, but my delight was in the hope of becoming pregnant. My heart and mind were not continually meditating on God's Word and His will for my life, but instead, on pregnancy tests and doctor's visits. The instant I opened my heart to a new direction—a direction I initially refused—God began to change my desires. The joy I found while seeking God's leading in adoption can only be described as a joy unspeakable. My words cannot adequately describe the feelings this journey has brought us and our entire family. In the end, God *did* grant me the desires of my heart, and He granted me even more than my mind could think to desire on my own. As I held my precious boy for the first time, I looked down and saw all God's grace in one tiny little face. I saw countless answered prayers of the faithful rising together with Zach and I as we stepped out in this leap of faith. I saw my husband's hand gently run his fingers through Jayden's hair, and I saw his face light up knowing he was now a father.

We knew we wanted to share our story with as many people as would listen. Our church was having a special Sunday school hour where we looked back at all the things God had done and blessed our church body with in the past year. Our Pastor asked if Zach and I would share our adoption story in about a 10-minute span. Zach did a beautiful job giving God the honor and glory for the things *He* had done. Here is just a portion of what he shared:

> For those of you who don't know, Leeann and I had the opportunity to adopt our little baby boy, Jayden Jonas Hale, this past November, about four months ago. We knew right away that this was something that

we wanted to share publicly if we ever got the chance to. We feel like God overwhelmingly poured His love, peace, mercy, grace, goodness and joy into our lives to where we can't help but overflow with praise and thanksgiving in our hearts. Today, instead of going over a timeline of events, I thought it would be more appropriate to share three ways that God has worked in our hearts to make us thankful. So, number one, we're thankful that God changed our hearts. Psalm 37:4 says, "Delight yourself in the LORD, and he will give you the desires of your heart." If you pursue God and you seek to know Him in a more deep and meaningful way, it's not that you'll get what you want, but that your heart will be shaped and molded by God, and your desires will start to align with His desires. And that's exactly what we saw throughout this adoption.

The second thing we are thankful for is the body of Christ, the church. One way we saw that support was through prayer. We had people coming to us every Sunday and Wednesday saying they were praying for us or asking how they could better pray for us, and hearing that day in and day out was so encouraging and helpful for us. We had so many things donated and so many gifts given. God has been so good in using His people to bless us. As far as things go financially, we were not in a position where we could afford adoption right away, and there are many people in this room who donated financially to us. I'm even thinking of one family in particular—I don't want to say their names because I think I would embarrass them—who wrote a huge check, and that was sacrificial giving because I know they don't have money just lying around. Things like that were just so special to us. We were able to cry with people in our sorrow and rejoice with those same people in our victory. This communicated to us that yeah, Leeann and I will be raising this child, but we're by far not the only ones who are invested in this kid's life. And this really isn't saying much, but Jayden is about 100 times more popular than I could ever dream of being, which is awesome! When I walk into the sanctuary, I see Leeann with Jayden and I just see a mob of people around her. Seeing how many people love this little boy already, that means a lot.

The last thing that we're thankful for is that adoption is such a beautiful picture of the gospel. The more I read my Bible and the more I think about adoption and what we've gone through with Jayden, the more I'm absolutely convinced that adoption is at the heart of the gospel.[4] There are so many parallels, so many similarities; I just want to share a few quickly. One, when we adopted Jayden, it was something that we planned. We were pursuing him before he was born. That reminds me of how God chose us, the elect, before the foundations of the world. Also, we know that adoption is a legal transaction, a once-and-for-all declaration. In a couple weeks, we're going to go before a judge who is going to declare Jayden a Hale. That gets my mind thinking about God, our judge, declaring us righteous because of the finished work of Jesus Christ on the cross. Lastly, for us to adopt Jayden, it was sacrificial; it was costly, both emotionally and

---

[4]   https://www.desiringgod.org/messages/adoption-the-heart-of-the-gospel

financially. When I think of the gospel, I think of the sacrifice that Jesus paid, and it was a costly sacrifice. We hope that Jayden will be a vehicle for us to share the gospel, to be salt and light in our community. I don't know if you guys have noticed, but Jayden looks a little bit different than me and Leeann. We think that's a good thing. We think that is a representation of how the gospel has no boundaries. And hopefully that will spark a lot of questions, and questions will give rise to an opportunity to share with strangers how our adoption process went, and how we're adopted as sons and daughters of God. Lastly, we hope Jayden will also be an opportunity to remind our church family and ourselves of these great biblical truths. One thing I enjoy about Pastor Joel is that he's always giving us object lessons, like a rock or a building block, so that we can have a tangible object to remind us of a spiritual truth. I hate to be a one-upper, but I think that Jayden is a much better version of that, and I hope that when you see him—hopefully not too long you'll see him running around—or you're holding him, or even if you say his name, that you think Jayden: that means Jehovah has heard; that means thankful. What a beautiful picture of how we're adopted into God's family and we're heirs with Christ.

So, we would just ask that you guys continue to be praying for us that we would be good stewards of what God has so graciously given us, that we would be wise with this gift. And we want to also say, if anyone has any questions or wants to talk with us about adoption, we would love to tell you more about our experience or tell you things we wish we did or didn't do. We would be more than happy to do that. And we're just really excited to see how God will use Jayden for His honor and glory.

20
A Once and for All Transaction

The months went on, and Jayden continued to grow healthy and strong. This once preemie baby was not looking so preemie anymore, and on March 24, 2017, we finalized our adoption before the judge. This finalization legally granted Zach and I to be Jayden's guardians and sole caregivers: his parents! A new birth certificate was created that had our names listed as the parents, and Jayden was now and forevermore our child, a Hale.

> Judge: "… and do you swear or affirm that the testimony you are about to give will be the truth, the whole truth, and nothing but the truth, so help you God?"
> Zach: "I do."
> Judge: "You may be seated."

Zach went on to answer some legality questions, including his date of birth, address, date of our marriage, and many more regarding Jayden.

> Attorney: "Can you tell the court about how Jayden has bonded with your family and why you would like to adopt him?"

As I mentioned before, my husband is not one to shed many tears, but Jayden had his daddy in tears before he could even answer the above question. This wasn't good because my testimony was to follow Zach's, and at that point, seeing my husband choke up in front of a courtroom of people because of his deep love for our baby brought the waterworks for me. The officer in the back of the courtroom must have seen me crying because as Zach continued to give his answer, the officer came up behind me and handed me a box of tissues. Through his tears, Zach gave his response.

Zach: "Um, these last four months have been really, really great with Jayden, watching him and just everything: seeing my wife care for him, loving that kid like I've never seen anyone love someone. We feel that God has made it abundantly clear that Jayden is the son for us, and that it's a great picture of us being adopted in Jesus Christ. We couldn't be happier. We love that kid so much."

Now, cue Leeann, the woman who has been up front crying since her husband swore under oath.

Judge: "... can you give your full name please?"
Leeann: "Leeann Marie Hale."

Again, I had to answer some background questions revolving around our case.

Attorney: "Do you understand that if the adoption is granted, the law will recognize Jayden the same as if he were your biological child?"
Leeann: "Yes!" *What a beautiful thing!*
Attorney: "Would you like to tell the court a little bit about your bond with Jayden and why you would like to adopt?"
Leeann: "My husband did a much better job than I would—*cue more tears.* Jayden is just the answer to so many prayers. And he

is loved by not just his mom and dad, but so many people have poured out so much love to him. And we just feel so blessed to have him in our life."

More talking, and more questions.

Judge: "Based upon my review of the file as well as the testimony presented today, ... I also find the adoption would be in the child's best interest, and that the child should be allowed to resume the name of Jayden Jonas Hale. Congratulations and good luck to both of ya."

That day, Jayden wasn't just adopted by Zach and me; he was adopted by a much larger group. So many people from around the globe were praying for Jayden before he was even born, and some were people we had never even met. People gave sacrificially to help bring him home; some sent cards and donated gifts, and some dedicated to praying daily for our baby. God used His people to bless us, whether it was crying with us in our sorrows or rejoicing with us in our victories. The outpouring of love we witnessed before—and now after Jayden's entrance to the world—is a beautiful picture of Jesus' love towards His children.

We firmly believe and are convinced that adoption is at the heart of the gospel. God chose and pursued us before the creation of the world. In the same way, we pursued Jayden before he ever reached our arms. Our finalization in court was a legal declaration, a once-and-for-all transaction. We stood before the judge and thought about God, our Judge, who will one day declare us righteous because of the finished work of Christ's death on the cross. We believe Jayden's life is a living example of God, our Father, adopting us as His children, and we look forward to sharing our story with as many people as will listen. Our God is a faithful God. He alone should receive all the honor and glory due His name.

21
Two Pink Lines

It was now Spring of 2018. Jayden was about 18 months old. What a joy he brought to our home with his giggles, the pitter-patter of his little feet, and sweet hugs and kisses. We felt so blessed. I wouldn't say I had given up hope, but the immense desire to become pregnant was no longer weighing on me day in and day out. We were not actively trying to become pregnant, but at the same time, we weren't doing anything to prevent it either. For the past month or so, Zach and I had started working with an attorney—the same one who finalized Jayden's adoption—and decided we were ready to start the adoption process once again. We were still in the early stages, but it was just as exciting as it was the first time around.

Zach had just left on a business trip for two days, and I really don't know what urged me to take a pregnancy test, but I did. I had a jumbo box of expired, cheap tests left over from our infertility journey a couple of years prior and decided to take the plunge. I waited the three minutes, still questioning why I was even doing this in the first place. I had absolutely no signs of morning sickness. Other than an odd, mid-cycle spotting lasting only a day or so, I had no reason to believe I was pregnant. And I didn't—I didn't believe it for a single second!

Ding dong, ding dong went my obnoxious alarm on my phone. I used to be waiting with bated breath every time it went off. This time I was much more lackadaisical. There really was no reason for me to think this was anything out of the ordinary—the ordinary being very irregular cycles one month after the next. I picked up the directions once more, as if I had somehow forgotten that two pink lines meant pregnant and one pink line meant not pregnant—complex stuff I was working with that morning, huh? I reached down to grab my urine-soaked stick and, to my astonishment, saw two pink lines! *Not possible!* I brought it closer to my eyes to make sure I wasn't seeing something that wasn't really there, but again, there were two pink lines, bright and vibrant, and plain as day.

"Oh my word, oh my word, oh my word! I'm pregnant. I'm pregnant!" The words came out of my mouth as the tears fell from my eyes, and I began to sink to the bathroom floor in astonishment. I think I almost put my dog, Sophie, in a panic attack because she began shaking and pacing in confused circles around our bathroom. Still in utter disbelief, I tried to convince myself that something must not be right. Come to think of it, that jumbo box of tests was expired, wasn't it? After all, I bought them pre-Jayden and Jayden was now over a year old. I knew what I had to do. A drugstore run was in order!

That day was my ladies' Bible study at church. Normally, I was rather rushed on Tuesday mornings to get Jayden fed and dressed, the diaper bag packed, and get out the door. *Forget my schedule-oriented, momma-mode today. I'm coming for you, Jayden. We're about to break our routine!* I ran in to wake Jayden up early and quickly got some breakfast in his tummy, then we headed to the drugstore for the expensive pregnancy test! Well, let's be honest, I'm still my frugal self, so I got the generic brand of the expensive one, but it still counts as being slightly reckless, right? I got home just in time to take another pregnancy test, and waited yet another three minutes to find out that there was indeed a baby growing in my belly. *I'm pregnant!*

Somehow, I still made it to Bible study early. I wanted to burst out the news to someone, *everyone,* but instead, I just kept my hands on my stomach and thanked God for the miracle growing inside me. During our time of praises and prayer requests that morning, my friend announced that they were expecting their third baby, and she was only about five weeks along. I had already done the math that morning, and I, too, was about five to six weeks along according to my calculations. That now made three ladies around the circle that morning who were expecting. Wait, make that four. I was just the only one who knew about number four.

The next couple of days were filled with joyful agony as I eagerly waited for Zach to return from his trip so I could share the exciting news. Throughout the day, I would find my hands caressing my stomach in awe of what was about to happen over the remaining eight months of this pregnancy, but I was still in shock that this was even happening.

Sharing the news with Zach on our bed Saturday morning was precious and sweet. He read a letter I had written that then led to him opening my pregnancy test—carefully sealed in a clear plastic bag. We embraced and I shared every detail I could remember. Life was so overwhelmingly thrilling. We were blessed, and God was good.

A few days later, my doctor's office was able to squeeze in an appointment for me. Apparently, it was customary that I take another pregnancy test before being seen. That was fine by me. My test at home was brilliant pink, so I was excited to be peeing on another stick and knew the outcome would be the same. As I sat with the nurse, answering routine questions and taking vitals, the time was up on my urine sample and she checked the strip.

"Was your home test pale in color?" she asked me.

Not knowing why she was asking, but proud as a peacock, I replied, "No, ma'am. It was bright pink."

"Okay," was all she replied.

Um... you can't just say okay and not give me something else to go off of. Why is she even asking me that?

"Is the test showing negative now?" I asked slightly concerned.

"I can see a line, but it's very, very faint. I wouldn't worry; the doctor will be able to take a better look." She tried to sound reassuring and positive, but I was starting to become concerned.

The doctor later told us that she couldn't find anything when she did the ultrasound. I asked what that meant and if she was concerned, hoping she would say something like, "Don't worry, this is all very normal. It's too early to see anything yet." But, along with a detailed description and a sympathetic, but matter-of-fact tone, she simply said, "I'm concerned. I should see something at this point, and I don't see anything." Honestly, I'm not sure if those were her exact words, but they were something along those lines. When I saw the look in her eyes, my body was present, but my mind was wandering. Everything was a hazy fog. I wanted to break down and cry right there on the table, but I held it in. I just sat there and nodded my head. Expressionless. Empty.

A couple other follow-up visits showed that there was no baby. No tiny miracle growing in my stomach, but an empty womb to caress as I went from complete and utter happiness with my first positive pregnancy test, to losing the baby in only a matter of days. *Why, God? Why would you give me this specific joy, only to tear it from my hands days later?* In my most honest and sincere thoughts with God, I was finally able to humbly say that it didn't matter if I never got pregnant.

Signing up for the adoption journey before we met Jayden, the Lord took hold of my heart and truly took the desire and longing I once had of becoming pregnant and replaced it with the deepest love you can imagine in adopting our precious son. Only God could truly take away the desires I once had of a natural pregnancy and replace them with true satisfaction and deep gratitude. I had no secret longings to one day deliver a baby from my own body, no secret times in prayer calling out to God to fill my womb. I was content! I was more than content. The more I learned about adoption, and then actually becoming a mom *through* adoption, the more I realized this was the path God had for me all along. And what a privilege it was to be chosen by God for this beautiful honor! I sincerely became fearful of becoming pregnant because I never wanted Jayden to think his life was a *means to an end.* I didn't want people coming up to me saying, "See, that's what God does. I knew you'd get pregnant after you adopted." The sounds of those words and many other phrases like it seemed so dirty to me. So cruel. I didn't adopt Jayden to *get pregnant.* I adopted Jayden because I loved him before I knew him. I loved him more than I loved myself. He was weak and helpless and his life *mattered,* not just to me, but to his birthmother who *chose* me, and most importantly, to his Heavenly Father who chose us all before the foundations of the earth. I adopted Jayden because he needed me, and I needed him. Before he was even born, I prayed for him. Before the creation of the world God knew that Jayden would be my son and I would be his mom; that's why I adopted Jayden, *because he's my son!*

My.

Son.

So why would God allow this pregnancy, create and stir up excitement in my heart, and then totally strip me of that joy? I didn't need it.

I didn't need a pregnancy to fulfill some desire in my heart. It wasn't something I needed to check off a hypothetical checklist. So why was God doing this? Why—only four months later—were we waiting for two days at the hospital for our second adoption only to find out that the birthmother changed her mind and decided to parent her baby. Why? Why does God allow such excruciating pain that cuts to the deepest, most tragic parts of our core? Isaiah 55:8-9 says, "For my thoughts are not your thoughts, neither are your ways my ways, declares the Lord. For as the heavens are higher than the earth, so are my ways higher than your ways and my thoughts than your thoughts."

My mere human speculations would never be able to grasp the thoughts of my Heavenly Father and I'm so thankful for that. Jenny— the same sweet, godly lady who encouraged me to pray out loud— once shared with me that if we could understand how and why God works, that would mean we serve a very small god. Instead, I serve a mighty God. I serve a God who doesn't think like my finite mind thinks and doesn't love like my selfish heart loves. This means even in my times of sowing in tears, I can reap with shouts of joy knowing my God is in control and I am not. My God walks before me and nothing comes as a surprise to Him. He wasn't shocked when I faced infertility struggles early in my marriage. He wasn't shocked when fertility treatments failed. He wasn't shocked when I had my miscarriage or when our second adoption fell through shortly after. And He wasn't shocked on August 13, 2018, when our second son, Jaxon Korbyn Hale, was born, and we were granted custody the following day. I was shocked. Zach was shocked. But God didn't even blink. For this reason, I choose to put my trust in a God who neither sleeps nor slumbers and who is working out *all* things for our good and His glory. In my pain and tears, God brought me Jayden and Jaxon. Without first sowing in tears, I would have never been in a position to cross paths with countless people, pray for two women so earnestly, love two little boys so fiercely, and reap the pure joy God has abundantly bestowed on my life.

Part Three: A Call to the Church

For just as the body is one and has many members, and all the members of the body, though many, are one body, so it is with Christ.

(1 Corinthians 12:12)

22
Unanswered Questions

"If 1 family in every 3 churches in the US adopted a waiting child, every waiting child in the US would have a forever family."[5] Let that statistic sink in for a second. How is it possible that there isn't at least one family in every three churches doing this already? James 1: 27 states, "Religion that is pure and undefiled before God the Father is this: to visit orphans and widows in their affliction, and to keep oneself unstained from the world." God commands us to care for orphans and widows; it's as simple as that. As Christians, we are not always called to a life of ease and comfort, but often to suffer for the sake of Christ. It has been my experience that in my times of suffering, my eyes have been drawn closer to my Savior. That's not because of any works of my own doing, but because of what Christ has done through me, and my prayer is that He has been glorified through those circumstances. This statistic should stir our hearts to the realization that the church needs to step up and care for those who can't care for themselves. My goal in writing this is not to be condescending in any way, or to come across as *holier than thou*, because, if you've made it this far in my book you know full well where I started. You saw my selfish heart that only God could change. However, my goal

---

5   http://www.abbafund.org/adoption-journey/adoption-facts/

is also to not be apologetic. I believe whole-heartedly that God has put this calling in my heart, and I need to be obedient to what I feel He has called me to say.

Adoption turns your world upside down; that's the cold, hard truth. It's hard; it's messy; it's painful; but it's the best decision that Zach and I have ever made. The amount of paperwork we had to complete was tedious and oftentimes overwhelming. Here is a list of all the forms and agency requirements we had to complete with the corresponding costs:

- Initial application with agency — $500
- Talk with one adoptive couple/complete the discussion form
- Complete at least 12 hours of adoption education
  - Read *The Connected Child* (4 credit hours)
  - Read 10 assigned adoption articles (4 credit hours)
  - Read *Adopted for Life* (4 credit hours)

- Complete the following forms:
  - Child Desired Form (3 pages)
  - Financial Information Statement (3 pages)
  - Leeann's Education Statement (2 pages)
  - Zach's Education Statement (2 pages)
  - Support Plan (2 pages)
  - Leeann's Questionnaire 1 (57 questions)
  - Zach's Questionnaire 1 (57 questions)
  - Leeann's Questionnaire 2 (276 questions)
  - Zach's Questionnaire 2 (276 questions)
  - Leeann's Out of State Child Abuse Form
  - Zach's Out of State Child Abuse Form
  - Domestic Home Study/Fee Agreement (2 pages)

- Duty to Disclose (1 page)
- Consent to Release Confidential Information (2 pages)
- Guardianship Information (1 page)
- Penalty of Perjury (1 page)
- Disclosure of Previous Home Studies (1 page)
- References to Call (1 page)
- Background Information (2 pages)
- Adoption Release and Consent (1 page)
- Attorney Intake Form (1 page)
- Agreement for Adoption Services (3 pages)
- Social Media (1 page)
- Adoption State Consents (7 pages)
- Responding to Complaints (2 pages)

- Leeann's Medical Report — $315
- Zach's Medical Report — $289
- Leeann's Fingerprinting — $50
- Zach's Fingerprinting — $50
- Attorney Fees — $3,772
- Placement Phase Fee — $6,000
- Orientation Phase Fee — $2,000
- Match Ready Phase Fee — $3,000
- Birthmother Fee (Payment 1) — $3,000 (This did not go straight to Jayden's birthmother, but was just what the agency called this fee phase.)
- Birthmother Fee (Payment 2) — $3,000
- At Match Phase Fee — $4,000
- Birthmother Relinquishment Fees — $1,000
- Home Study Fee — $1,550
- 14 copies of Shutterfly profile books — $253.62

- Two-visit home study interview (pre-adoption)
- One-visit home study interview (post adoption)

Reading this list can be somewhat exhausting and maybe even intimidating. Why are the requirements for a stable, loving family so extensive? Why are there so many obstacles to overcome in adopting while babies are regularly born into abusive or drug-filled homes? The only response I can give is: *I don't know.* But the beauty is, I don't have to know the answer to that question. God is sovereign over the entire world; who am I to question Him? We live in a day where we want answers to problems immediately. If something doesn't make sense in our finite minds, we need an explanation. Adoption leads you down a path of countless unanswered questions. However, in my experience, God replaced those unanswered questions with a faith that could only come from Him. I was strengthened in my questions because I learned to rely on a God who held all the answers.

Adoption forces you to step into a world of unknowns, and where there are unknowns, therein lies faith. I can't tell you why it's so easy for some mothers to bring children into a world of poverty and abuse, and I can't tell you why loving couples who put God first in their lives are required to go through such a rigorous check-off list for the chance that someone may choose them to be parents. My intent with this list was not to complain about the rules and financial requirements for adoptive parents, but to be open and honest about the process. I was inclined to say that adoption is not for the faint of heart, but now I question if maybe that's exactly who it is for. Prior to stepping into the world of adoption, I had never been more faint of heart. I was broken, weary, sorrow-stricken, and deeply wrestling with God's leading in my life. However, my faintness was overcome as I grew in my faith. I learned to rely on my gracious Heavenly Father who showed Himself faithful in my times of doubt and uncertainty.

From talking to family and friends, these are common questions I hear: *Why is it so much work? Why do they* (adoption agencies) *make it so hard? Why is it so much money? How do you know if a birthmother is lying to you about her health? How do you know if the birthmother is just using you for money?* My question back would be: *Why does it matter?* Asking those questions just gives way to doubt and makes it easy to give an excuse to close your door and pass on an opportunity to make an orphan a son or daughter. I don't mean to sound as if I'm naïve and don't see the potential danger in some of those scenarios, but if we allow ourselves to be scared off by every red flag linked with adoption, no child would ever know a home. The truth is, from the day you sign up to adopt, *unknowns* will always stand in the way. You may never know the full medical history of a child's birth family. Our birthmothers were never subject to lie detector tests or drug tests proving they didn't consume any alcohol or illegal substances during their pregnancies. There isn't a one hundred percent chance of knowing if a birthmother is just using you to gain some type of financial aid. You will be inconvenienced more times than you can count with all the paperwork, appointments and invoices. And *questions* will be the hovering, dark cloud following you at every turn. But God! Brothers and sisters in Christ, be encouraged that you serve a God who knows the answers to every question in every circumstance. He is preparing you for the task He has set before you.

When we had our first failed match, I was devastated. In my heart, I felt that baby was my son before he was even born. I prayed for him. I prayed for his birthparents. I prayed ceaselessly sitting in the hospital waiting room for two days just waiting to see his sweet face and hold his tiny frame. When our attorney sat us down to prepare us for the fact that it was quite possibly going to result in a failed match, she told me something I will never forget. She told us that she couldn't explain why these types of situations happen, but she had to believe they happen for a reason. Her advice wasn't anything complex, but it impacted me greatly.

You see, at the time of the birth of this baby, the birthparents had told no one in their family or circle of friends about the pregnancy. The birthmother felt she would be shunned by her mother if she ever found out and thought it best to just keep it a secret. Her life, at the time, was falling apart. She didn't have a job, she was no longer in a relationship with the baby's father, and she didn't have much money to her name. She was emotionally breaking down and suffering deeply within. If God didn't present this situation to us, I would have never had the opportunity to pray for her. And if Zach and I weren't praying for her, who was? Most likely, no one. No one would have known her situation, and no one would have held her up tirelessly in prayer. I still think of her and her baby from time to time, and when I do, I say an extra prayer for her. I later found out that she called her mom from the hospital room after her baby was born and explained everything to her. She wasn't shunned by her mother but welcomed with open arms. I don't know how her story will unfold, but I pray that God would unite and strengthen the bonds of that family and that God would be the center of their lives. I pray the sweet baby boy would grow to know and love the Lord with all his heart and live to serve Him faithfully.

Is adoption expensive? Absolutely! That is exactly why I included all our expenses with the list. Is adoption time-consuming? Definitely! That's why I included every single paper we had to complete. Is adoption an emotional roller coaster? Completely! Adoption has highs so high you think you'll never be able to utter a sentence without crying tears of joy again, and for some, it also carries lows so low you begin to question if this is really the path God has for your life.

Zach and I didn't sign up with an extra twenty-something grand in our back pockets.[6] We signed up with a whole lot of faith in our God who called us to this mission. We didn't have all the money up front, but what we did have, and what we still have, is a faithful God. Philippians 1:6 reads, "And I am sure of this, that he who began a good work in you will bring it to completion at the day of Jesus Christ." Brothers and sisters in Christ, I urge you to tune in to God's calling in your life. Don't let *your* will for your life speak so loudly that you can't hear *God's* will.

---

[6] Our second adoption through an attorney was significantly less expensive—less than half the cost of our agency fees. Seek different options. Usually attorneys are the less expensive route, but make sure they are well-qualified. Look into the Federal adoption tax credit as well. The only reason we were able to complete our second adoption so quickly was because the costs were completely covered by the tax credit we received from our first adoption. Finding the initial money up front is the challenging part, but if you can make it work on the front end, the financial benefits on the back end make it possible to either pay off your first adoption, or start the process a second time.

23
Comments and Assumptions

If you've been around our family or seen our picture, you will notice that our boys don't look like us. They don't have my pale skin decorated with freckles, and they don't have their dad's straight-as-a-board brunette hair. Instead, they have beautiful, dark eyes, tight, black curls and rich milk-chocolate-colored skin. There will probably never be a day when someone comes up to me and says, "My, your boys are the spitting image of you." *That's not a bad thing!* God's family looks nothing alike, and I love that my family reminds me of my Heavenly Father's family daily. I was in the grocery store one day and a lady stocking the shelves looked over because she heard Jayden making noises in the shopping cart.

"Is he yours, or are you babysitting?" she asked very straightforwardly.

"Yes, ma'am. He's my son," I replied.

"He doesn't look mix to me," was her immediate and very confused response.

What a perfect open door for me to share the blessing that God had given our family through adoption. This conversation with the kind stock lady is just one of many that Zach and I have had since bringing Jayden and Jaxon into our home. People look, and people have questions. Hearing these kinds of comments or getting the occasional confused look doesn't make us feel uncomfortable or hurt our feelings—most of the time. Instead it brings a smile to our faces because even though our boys are still so young, we can see God using each of them to bring glory to His name. I believe one of the greatest gifts we can be given as parents is to see our children shine for Christ in the midst of a very dark world.

When I found out that Zach and I were the *only* family in our state—with our agency, at the time of Jayden's adoption—open to an all African American baby, I was so angry. Keep in mind, we were working with a Christian-based agency. I questioned how any couple that claimed to know and love the Lord would specifically mark on their "Child Desired" form that they did not want a black baby. *How dare they?!* When we went through the adoption process a couple of years later with Jaxon, I found the same thing to be true. We weren't working with a Christian agency like before, but we were working with a local attorney who had a diverse range of couples. I found out that a lot of couples are open to the idea of a biracial baby, just not one who is fully African American. And some couples who are open to a biracial baby are not willing to have any mix with African American. After my anger wore off, I was left with confusion and sadness. I don't write this because I'm a *white* mom to two *black* boys, I write this because I'm a *mom* to my *boys*. I looked in the eyes of my sweet, beautiful baby boy and wondered how someone could say no to him because his skin didn't match the color of theirs. It didn't make any sense to me. It never will make sense to me. But it made me realize that in this world our boys will face certain prejudices that I will never face in my lifetime. As parents, it's going to be our job to teach them to rise above the cruelty of this world and replace hatred with a Christ-like love. It will be our job to remind them that when this world tries to pull them under, they are loved by a Heavenly King who has promised to never leave or forsake them. It is our job to instill in them characteristics that will make them the men God created them to be.

Why is race even an option when considering adoption? I know of people who have walked the path of adoption with the mindset of finding a baby who shares their exact skin color and not a shade darker or lighter. I have also had others tell me that if they were to adopt, that's exactly what they would do, too. *These are believers!* Where is the love that God commands of His children?

Ephesians 4:2-3: "*[W]ith all humility and gentleness, with patience, bearing with one another in love, eager to maintain the unity of the Spirit in the bond of peace.*"

John 13:34: "*A new commandment I give to you, that you love one another: just as I have loved you, you also are to love one another.*"

Matthew 22:36-39: "*'Teacher, which is the great commandment in the Law?' And he said to him, 'You shall love the Lord your God with all your heart and with all your soul and with all your mind. This is the great and first commandment. And the second is like it: You shall love your neighbor as yourself.'*"

1 John 3:18: "*Little children, let us not love in word or talk but in deed and in truth.*"

Take yourself back to the time when Jesus roamed the earth in His sinless, human form. Recall the verse in Matthew 19:14: "[B]ut Jesus said, 'Let the little children come to me and do not hinder them, for to such belongs the kingdom of heaven.'" At the time, the disciples did not want Jesus to be bothered by such little children so they tried turning them away. Jesus rebuked them and called the children to gather around Him. Jesus didn't specify what children He wanted; He wanted *all* the children to be able to gather around Him to hear

His teachings. What I'm saying isn't anything new, but it's a simple truth I feel is being ignored.

Revelation 7:9 says, "After this I looked, and behold, a great multitude that no one could number, from every nation, from all tribes and peoples and languages, standing before the throne and before the Lamb, clothed in white robes, with palm branches in their hands." This verse clearly states that people of *all* colors will be in heaven together. If you believe the Bible, you have to believe that God adopted people of *every* tribe and *every* nation as His sons and daughters. Let's call that our "Premise A." These same Bible-believing people would also agree that we should strive to be more like Christ in our daily walk: "Therefore be imitators of God, as beloved children. And walk in love, as Christ loved us and gave himself up for us, a fragrant offering and sacrifice to God" (Ephesians 5:1-2). We'll call that "Premise B." So if A and B are true—which they are, because Scripture undoubtedly supports both premises—then as followers of Christ, we must also walk in love, not showing favoritism for any one race as we follow God's leading in the adoption process. It's as simple as that!

As a mother of two boys with whom I do not share my genetic makeup, I often get questions, and two in particular sting to my core. I must remind myself that ignorance does not necessarily equate with hatred and that my actions and my responses are constantly on display to those around me. A conversation that I recently had at the grocery store checkout line was a true test of my testimony. As the cashier was ringing up my items, another customer pushed her cart up behind mine and immediately interrupted our conversation with, "Oh, they are so cute. Are they yours?" That morning, in particular, I was feeling frustrated that I had to once again answer this question. At times, I wished that others would just assume my boys are mine like any other mother walking into the grocery store with her children. But understanding the customer's obvious—and, I suppose, valid—confusion, I politely smiled and responded with a simple "Yes," and tried to end the conversation with that. God must have known I needed to put this chapter in my book, so He allowed this lady to push every last button I had and continue to give me the third degree about my boys. I'll only hit on the highlights and spare you the rest.

"Are they brothers?" she continued. I always immediately answer yes to this question, because they *are*. I know exactly what people mean when they ask this, but my answer is still the same. They want to know if they are *biologically* related, and I want to communicate how much that *doesn't matter*. So, the follow-up from her was, of course, "Well, I mean *real* brothers, I know they are brothers..." Let me explain how hurtful this is for a mother to hear. I understand our family did not come together in the most conventional way, but that doesn't mean my family isn't still a *family* in every sense of the word. From the second our boys' birthmothers chose us to parent these two precious boys, they were our children and we were a family. Just because my boys do not share the same genetics as my husband and I, or each other, that doesn't make us any less of a family. Just because my boys have different birthmothers, that doesn't mean they aren't real brothers. DNA doesn't make a family. My boys are real brothers and we are a real family.

The woman continued her endless stream of questions: "Oh, so ya'll decided to adopt instead of have kids of your own? Are you going to adopt again?" At that point, I knew I was in for a real treat with this woman so I just let her continue and prayed the Lord would hold my tongue. If the brother question wasn't enough, she decided to give me my final favorite—insert sarcasm here—question. "Maybe try for a girl next time?" I cannot adequately describe in writing how much this comment rattles my insides. *Try for a girl*? First of all, if I was pregnant, is there some special juice I'm not aware of that produces a specific gender of your choosing? Second, no I'm not *trying* for a girl, and I never will. For the same reason I will never *try* for a boy. With each adoption, we allowed God to be the deciding factor of what child He would allow to join our family, in the same way that He would be the deciding factor if I became pregnant. A family is not truly complete by simply having one child of each gender. I'm not missing out on special joys or blessings that only come with girls, just like a family of all girls isn't missing out on any specific blessings or joys by not having a boy. I never want my boys to grow up hearing that question and wondering, *Would Mommy be happier if she had a girl?* No, Mommy wouldn't be happier! Mommy would be the exact same level of happiness if God added to our family no matter the gender.

Since adding to our family through adoption, I became very protective of our boys' birthmothers. I didn't like it when people would make comments and assumptions like, *How could someone give up their baby? I guess she probably was on lots of drugs or something. I don't understand what she could be thinking. The baby will be better off with you.* Experiencing adoption firsthand changes the way you view certain things, and for me, many of the changes came in the area of our birthmother. Our birthmother was not some druggie on the street who couldn't care for her child; she was a strong woman who loved her child so much that she wanted the best life for him. Not all birthmothers have a clean medical history during the life of their pregnancy. Some, unfortunately, do not care for their bodies properly and, in turn, put their babies at risk unnecessarily. As painful and difficult as that idea is to grasp, as adoptive parents, we need to rise above society's negative perception that only aims to shame the child's birthmother. The child is the only one harmed if he grows to believe that he came from a terrible woman who never loved or wanted him. Instead, find the good, even if you have to dig down deep to find it, while at the same time remaining completely honest. For example, at age-appropriate intervals, you could share with your child that his birthmother did indeed make mistakes. You could explain that sometimes people's pain becomes so overpowering they begin to search for happiness anywhere they can find it. Instead of turning to Christ who is the only source of true happiness, they turn to alcohol or drugs, or whatever else it may be. You could further explain that any type of substance abuse takes control of one's mind and causes them to do things they know they shouldn't do, and at some level do not even want to do. The pull of addiction is something we can't truly understand or pass judgement on from the outside looking in. It's important to be honest with our children, but it's also important they grow to know they are loved deeply. It's important they know that the choices their birthmother made were very wrong and dangerous, but at the same time, in every case there is hope because there is God. Whether the birthmother was an addict, a scared teenage girl, or a middle-aged woman, there is always hope and there is always a way to make sure the child grows to know he was *not* a mistake. Women who choose to carry their baby through the entire pregnancy and then place the baby for adoption are to be encouraged rather than shamed.

I understand that the majority of the comments I just spoke of often stem from good intentions by well-meaning people. I also would be the first to admit that before I walked the path of adoption, I either spoke or thought some of the exact same words that now cause my whole body to cringe when I hear them spoken to me. Part of the reason I added this final section in my book was to create an awareness. I wanted to share our joys because our adoption experience has truly given me a reason to shout from the rooftops how blessed I am to be the mother to my precious sons. I wanted to share our sorrow because I didn't earn the title "Mom" without a deep-rooted pain that I know many women suffer silently. And I wanted to share the negative comments and assumptions because I want to raise my boys in a world where adoption is understood and valued.

24

Rise Up

◇

Church, it's time to rise up! Stop telling God what you are and are not going to do. Stop giving excuses for why you can't play a part in adoption. Stop saying, *Adoption is great, but it's not for our family.* It's time to rise up, brothers and sisters in Christ. It's time to show the love of Christ to the fatherless. There are many ways you can help; you must only have a willing heart. Below I have compiled just a few examples of how you can help. Pray over this list, and ask God where He is calling you to serve.

- Adopt a child.
- Become a foster parent.
- Help a family put together a fundraiser for their adoption.
  - Have children raise money (bake sales, lemonade stands, etc.)
  - Yard sales
  - Auctions: Volunteer items free of charge for the adoptive family to auction off. This is a great opportunity for small businesses to get their name out for advertisement at the same time.

- Chick-fil-A Night: Some locations will allow the proceeds for a specific night and time slot to go towards your adoption costs. It's a great way to invite all your friends to come together for good food while helping an adoptive family.
- Pancake breakfast/spaghetti supper (or any variation): Sell tickets and get volunteers to pitch in for the cost of food.
- T-shirt sales

- Be a prayer warrior for a family in the adoption/foster process.
- Volunteer at a local pregnancy center.
- Contribute financially to an adoptive family.
- Throw a baby shower.
- Send letters of encouragement during the time of waiting.
- Pray over the couple as they wait.
- Sponsor a child.

  - Our church partners with an outreach called Remember. Part of this outreach includes an orphanage in Burma. Many of these children are left without parents due to persecution in poverty-stricken countries. You can sponsor a child for $30 a month, volunteer to participate in mission trips, or help contribute financially to someone going on the trip (http://www.rememberthose.org/).

These are just some practical ways that you can contribute to adoption. Get off the sidelines and get in the game; these children need our help! Watch God work in mighty ways as you trade out your comfortable lifestyle to give a child a home and a family.

The following chart[7] breaks down the number of waiting children and the number of churches by state. If this doesn't stir our hearts to action, I honestly don't know what will. We need to move our focus off of the comforts this life brings and onto the life-altering, beautiful challenges that come with adoption. Where there is pain and struggle, there is also abundant rewards and immeasurable love. It's true what they say, adoption turns your life upside down. But if that's the case, I don't ever want to be right side up again. Adoptive families, I urge you to continue to trust God as you sow in tears and look forward to reaping with shouts of joy! God is at work; we must only obey His call.

---

[7]   http://www.s444086331.onlinehome.us/consideringadoption/waitingkidsinyourstate/

State	Children Waiting FY 2014*	Churches*
Alabama	1,027	10,760
Alaska	704	1,050
Arizona	3,641	3,771
Arkansas	1,034	6,343
California	14,098	22,798
Colorado	1,008	3,813
Connecticut	1,227	2,909
Delaware	202	1,009
District of Columbia	243	825
Florida	5,558	16,805
Georgia	1,983	14,380
Hawaii	187	1,163
Idaho	322	1,776
Illinois	2,854	13,097
Indiana	2,731	9,204
Iowa	1,050	4,766
Kansas	2,116	4,615
Kentucky	2,420	6,859
Louisiana	1,033	7,983
Maine	590	1,539
Maryland	464	5,816
Massachusetts	2,771	4,039
Michigan	3,584	11,169
Minnesota	1,188	5,628
Mississippi	1,184	7,718
Missouri	2,325	8,973
Montana	587	1,518
Nebraska	690	2,595
Nevada	2,059	1,248
New Hampshire	159	1,033
New Jersey	2,593	6,713
New Mexico	990	1,796
New York	5,463	14,767

North Carolina	2,416	17,625
North Dakota	262	1,252
Ohio	2,942	14,657
Oklahoma	3,975	6,737
Oregon	1,783	3,646
Pennsylvania	1,896	15,539
Rhode Island	212	703
South Carolina	1,211	9,479
South Dakota	336	1,368
Tennessee	2,652	11,179
Texas	13,238	27,505
Utah	629	2,582
Vermont	232	692
Virginia	1,532	10,952
Washington	3,213	5,393
West Virginia	1,388	3,432
Wisconsin	1,147	6,045
Wyoming	81	803
Puerto Rico	688	
Total	**107,918**	**348,067**

Our first meeting with fertility specialists, one of many doctor visits.

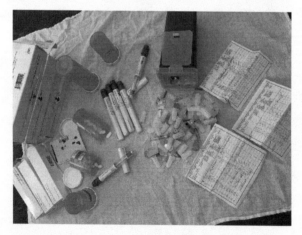

My medications from fertility treatments.

Our first meeting with our adoption agency.

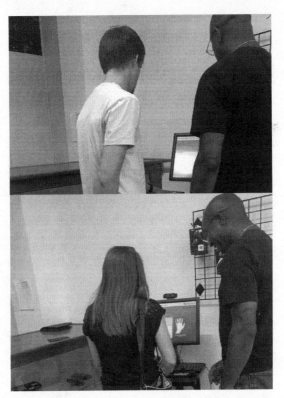

Zach and I getting fingerprinted.

Our praying friends gave us the beautiful bouquet of flowers that decorated our table for our home study.

The two chairs on the right were where Zach and I sat in the waiting room of the hospital and waited for the news on Jayden.

We were so excited to hold Jayden for the very first time.

Gifts from my Greenville shower—most of the
bags are double and triple stacked.

Jayden was about a month old at our post-adoption home study.

Another picture from Jayden's post-adoption home study.

Jayden's finalization.

My war room.

The Giugliano family (left) was at the airport bringing their son home for the first time. The Riley family (right) finalized the adoption of their son with the same judge, in the same courtroom, with the same attorney, and on the same morning that we finalized our adoption with Jayden.

Family of three. Jayden was about 18 months old.

Holding Jaxon for the first time in our hospital room.

Jaxon's finalization.

One of the first pictures as a family of four. Jayden—almost
2 years old; Jaxon—1 month old (September 2018).

Jayden—almost 2 years old; Jaxon—2 months old (October 2018).

Me with my two boys a couple of days after
Jaxon's finalization (November 2018).

Jayden—almost 3 years old; Jaxon—1 year old (September 2019).

Scripture from My War Room

"For this child I prayed, and the LORD has granted me my petition that I made to him" (1 Samuel 1:27).

"Sing praises to the LORD, O you his saints, and give thanks to his holy name. For his anger is but for a moment, and his favor is for a lifetime. Weeping may tarry for the night, but joy comes with the morning" (Psalm 30:4-5).

"Hear my cry, O God, listen to my prayer; from the end of the earth I call to you when my heart is faint. Lead me to the rock that is higher than I, for you have been my refuge, a strong tower against the enemy" (Psalm 61:1-3).

"The LORD is high above all nations, and his glory above the heavens! Who is like the LORD our God, who is seated on high, who looks far down on the heavens and the earth? He raises the poor from the dust and lifts the needy from the ash heap, to make them sit with princes, with the princes of his people. He gives the barren woman a home, making her the joyous mother of children. Praise the LORD!" (Psalm 113:4-9)

"Those who sow in tears shall reap with shouts of joy! He who goes out weeping, bearing the seed for sowing, shall come home with shouts of joy, bringing his sheaves with him" (Psalm 126:5-6).

"The LORD will fulfill his purpose for me; your steadfast love, O LORD, endures forever. Do not forsake the work of your hands" (Psalm 138:8).

"For you formed my inward parts; you knitted me together in my mother's womb. I praise you, for I am fearfully and wonderfully made. Wonderful are your works; my soul knows it very well. My frame was not hidden from you, when I was being made in secret, intricately woven in the depths of the earth" (Psalm 139:13-15).

"The plans of the heart belong to man, but the answer of the tongue is from the LORD" (Proverbs 16:1).

"And blessed is she who believed that there would be a fulfillment of what was spoken to her from the Lord" (Luke 1:45).

"I write these things to you who believe in the name of the Son of God, that you may know that you have eternal life. And this is the confidence that we have toward him, that if we ask anything according to his will he hears us. And if we know that he hears us in whatever we ask, we know that we have the requests that we have asked of him" (1 John 5:13-15).

"Rejoice in hope, be patient in tribulation, be constant in prayer" (Romans 12:12).

"So we do not lose heart. Though our outer self is wasting away, our inner self is being renewed day by day. For this light momentary affliction is preparing for us an eternal weight of glory beyond all comparison, as we look not to the things that are seen but to the things that are unseen. For the things that are seen are transient, but the things that are unseen are eternal" (2 Corinthians 4:16-18).

"But the fruit of the Spirit is love, joy, peace, patience, kindness, goodness, faithfulness, gentleness, self-control; against such things there is no law" (Galatians 5:22-23).

"[T]hat according to the riches of his glory he may grant you to be strengthened with power through his Spirit in your inner being, so that Christ may dwell in your hearts through faith—that you, being rooted and grounded in love, may have strength to comprehend with all the saints what is the breadth and length and height and depth, and to know the love of Christ that surpasses knowledge, that you may be filled with all the fullness of God" (Ephesians 3:16-19).

"And I am sure of this, that he who began a good work in you will bring it to completion at the day of Jesus Christ" (Philippians 1:6).

"[D]o not be anxious about anything, but in everything by prayer and supplication with thanksgiving let your requests be made known to God. And the peace of God, which surpasses all understanding, will guard your hearts and your minds in Christ Jesus" (Philippians 4:6-7).

"Count it all joy, my brothers, when you meet trials of various kinds, for you know that the testing of your faith produces steadfastness. And let steadfastness have its full effect, that you may be perfect and complete, lacking in nothing" (James 1:2-4).

Resources

Adoption facts. (n.d.). Retrieved from https://www.abbafund.org/adoption-journey/adoption-facts/

Claiming the federal adoption tax credit for 2019. (2019). Retrieved from https://www.nacac.org/help/adoption-tax-credit/adoption-tax-credit-2019

Dempsey, R., A. Storm, & J. Mann (Hosts). (2016, July 7). Anthony and Jennifer talk about adoption [Radio interview]. In J. Mann, *HIS Morning Crew*. Greenville, SC: HIS Radio.

Ingram, J., M. Redman, & T. Wanstall. (2011). Never once [Recorded by Matt Redman]. On 10000 reasons [CD]. Eastbourne, England: Kingsway Music.

Kendrick, A. (Director), & Kendrick, S. & G. Wheeler (Producers). (2015). *War room* [Film]. United States: Kendrick Brothers Productions.

Moore, R. (2015). *Adopted for life: the priority of adoption for Christian families and churches* (2nd ed.). Wheaton, IL: Crossway.

Piper, J. (2007, February 10). Adoption: the heart of the gospel. Retrieved from https://www.desiringgod.org/messages/adoption-the-heart-of-the-gospel

Purvis, K. B., D. R. Cross, & W. L. Sunshine. (2007). *The connected child: bring hope and healing to your adoptive family*. New York, NY: McGraw Hill.

Remember. (2019). Retrieved from http://www.rememberthose.org/

Waiting kids in your state. (n.d.). Retrieved from http://www.s444086331.
onlinehome.us/consideringadoption/waitingkidsinyourstate/

Contact Leeann at:

Website—https://www.facebook.com/sowingintearsbook

Email—sowingintearsbook@gmail.com